Right Person/Right Relationship

A Practical Guide to Prepare for and Find Your Great Relationship

By Jill Early, BSW

Relationship Coach

Jill Early's Right Person/Right Relationship
A Practical Guide to Prepare for and Find Your Great Relationship

Scripture references /quotes, unless otherwise noted, are from The Holy Bible, Updated New American Standard Version, the New International Version, and the American Standard Version.

Editing and Coaching provided by Denise Michaels, International Book Writing Guild. mentoringwithdenise@gmail.com ibwguild.com
Cover design and Book Formatting produced by Julie Azhadi

Published June 2021
ISBN# 9798514659630

DEDICATION

Dedicated to Olivia and Elaina, who make my first relationship attempt unequivocally worthwhile.

And to Samantha, my young counseling intern friend, who said she would read a book like this if I wrote it, so I did.

ACKNOWLEDGEMENTS

Many thanks and much appreciation go to my husband who had to keep hearing about this book but wasn't allowed to read it, and my wonderful bestie Sharon who was the first to painstakingly read every word and bravely share her opinions. I couldn't have gotten this new adventure off the ground without my awesome editor and coach, Denise Michaels, or my wonderful friend, Julie Azhadi, who worked so tirelessly to make the book beautiful and helped me through so much of the technical stuff, or Delaney and Patch Mahoney who enabled me to connect with the world, and look my best doing it. I am constantly amazed and grateful for author and international speaker Robert Cialdini's guidance, support, and encouragement. Getting past "Go" would have been so much harder without his help. Special thanks and love go to Hanae for making me an international author!

There has been so much help along this whole-new adventure, and I'm so appreciative to everyone who encouraged and supported me. You know who you are, and I'm so grateful to you!

My full acknowledgment and gratitude go to God for creating us, Jesus for loving me enough to walk all this way with me, and the sweet Spirit who lifted my head. I believe this book is God's words, my typing. I had such fun—mostly—writing this with Him!

Table of Contents

INTRODUCTION

We're messing up. We simply don't know how to have the relationships and connectedness we're made for and so desperately need. We look in the wrong places, present ourselves poorly, accept far less than what we deserve and then the relationship we patch together implodes. We wonder why for a few days (hours?) then we start the whole process again. You can do better. You're reading this book, so I assume you want to do better. Come along with me for the next 25 chapters, and let's see if together we can radically improve the trajectory of your relationships.

What is a relationship, anyway? What are we even talking about? The type of relationship I'm talking about in this book is probably more along the lines of a man/woman close relationship that could lead to marriage, but the principles and skills you'll read really could transfer to any close friendship as well. The bottom line is connection to another human being. I'm talking about feeling that trust and safe vulnerability that we all yearn for, and the joy and ease of just being with a person to whom we feel connected, the give/take, the listening/talking and laughing and shared experience that make life so much more valuable. It is HARD to connect; connection requires one not-perfect human to bond with another not-perfect-in-other-ways human. Lots of potential for discord.

There are three major components to any good, close relationship --Right Person and Right Relationship. Wait, you say. That's only two, you protest. No, no, my reading friend— "Right person" doesn't just refer to FINDING the right person. You also must BE the right person. So now we're back to three.

There's only been one truly perfect human relationship recorded in the history of humans for us to use as our example—the one God created in Adam and Eve, before it got irrevocably messed up. Look in your Bible (please have one!) at the story of Eve and Adam (It's in Genesis 2. Probably Page 2 in your Bible), and you will see that Eve was created because God didn't want Adam to be alone because he needed a helper. (I'm pretty sure God knew what He was doing here—if He had made Eve first, she probably wouldn't have needed a helper! Women tend to be more capable and independent when it comes to daily life things, like finding the mayonnaise in the fridge, etc.). Beyond simply needing a helper, though, God knew it simply wasn't good for man to be isolated. Humans need other humans. So He caused Adam to fall into a deep sleep, maybe with lots of turkey and mashed potatoes as a sleep aid, and created Eve from one of Adam's ribs. You've probably heard the lovely story of how God made her from a rib so she could be close to Adam's heart, from his side so he could protect her, and so on. I don't know about that. Maybe God just decided man could spare a rib—I'll pause here for just a moment while you enjoy the spare/rib pun. Okay.—and He figured that was as good a place as any to star

Whatever the Divine thinking was, Eve was created, and thus the too-brief perfect human relationship began. Adam immediately declared his appreciation of her and his awareness that she was part of him. They were one (v.2:24) person with two unique, perfectly complementary bodies, minds, emotions, and abilities. Since God personally planted a garden in which He placed the man (Gen 2:7), His most prized creation who He actually breathed His perfect breath into, no doubt the garden was beyond beautiful, lush and fun. God is, by the way, the awesome creator of fun. Though the Bible doesn't really say so, I'm sure Adam and Eve had an amazingly joyful time frolicking in this perfect garden, playing in the rivers (Gen. 2:10) which probably held the most sparkling water ever and climbing the huge trees and enjoying the beauty that was made just for them. They probably giggled when squirrels bounced into trees, chased bunnies, and generally enjoyed the beauty around them as well as each other. They had no shame (v.2:25) and since they were joined as one and each was created in perfection, there was no arrogance, greed, pride, malice, or baggage. There was no reason or room for meanness.

Then, sadly, sin slid in and suddenly the perfect relationship was perfect no more. There's no way to know how long the time of perfection lasted. It totals 9 verses which, I suppose, could be a few hours or many years, but the fact is that it came to a crashing end. Adam and Eve went against the instruction they were given by the Creator. At least for a moment they were in this mess together. They saw for the first time their nakedness and together began sewing fig leaves which really was a two-person job, since they had a lot of figuring out to do because sewing was never needed before and there was no Hobby Lobby to supply needles and thread. They also, presumably, decided together to hide from God. So, they were partners in crime,-- still one person, but a guilty and very broken one.

Then, it got even worse. God asked Adam to explain what's up and Adam immediately shoots the blame for the whole mess onto Eve. He might as well have shot a cannon at her. Eve was left unguarded, unprotected, and betrayed for the first time ever. The same guy who said "She's the bone of my bone and flesh of my flesh" (v. 2:23) was suddenly arrogantly saying "Hey, I dunno. I'm a victim. She did it all. You deal with her; she's got it coming to her!" and then he sat back and let Eve take the rap by herself. The one became two. Think about it; everything in the perfect relationship changed. Eve and Adam already suffered from this new thing called shame or at least an awareness of their nakedness (v. 3:7). They had to quickly scramble to escape the embarrassment from nakedness which wasn't even an issue a very short time ago. They stepped away from what their Maker intended, and shame trotted right into the picture. The broken became shattered. Humankind was forever weakened.

What was it about being naked that caused so much disruption and warrants a significant part of the story of mankind's break from God and one another? Verse 7 tells us that after eating what they were not to eat, their eyes were opened and they felt an immediate need to cover themselves, but why? Their disobedience happened when they arrogantly pursued the wisdom of knowing what they were warned to never know, but how did this translate into immediately covering their loins? The general assumption is because they were ashamed, but the text doesn't say that nor does it explain why they would feel ashamed of having different body parts. Obviously in today's world it would be shameful and grossly inappropriate to go around with no clothing, but that was all Adam and Eve knew, so where did the sudden need to cover up come from? I imagine they noticed the differences in their bodies all along, but it wasn't anything of importance until they understood their separateness, their differences. It could have been that, once their eyes were open, they no longer wanted to see the other person's nakedness, but it seems more likely to me that they had a new, unpleasant sense of their own vulnerabilities and need to protect themselves at all costs. Their eyes that could now see both good and evil, and they could no longer simply be. No longer could they simply be with each other and their Creator. There were barriers that weren't there before like differences and pitfalls and rules, and it took root not in the fruit or the garden, but within themselves. Since it's impossible to outwardly cover our most vulnerable parts like our emotions, our sense of value, and more, they covered what once was exposed without thought or fear. They placed a barrier between what once joined the two together with perfect ease and accessibility.

Because they chose to "do themselves" rather than follow God's guidance, God then was forced to give Adam and Eve the consequences they earned. There are several consequences of this fall, but for our purposes the focus is the curse of women forever having a desire for their husbands (v. 3:16).

For years I didn't understand this as a curse. I thought "Oh, that is sweet. Women will always desire their husbands and won't get tired of them or bored or something, so this is a good thing, right?" Nooo. I've since realized no one desires what they already have. I have a car, so there's no need for me to desire one. I might desire a newer or better car, but there's no reason I'd desire an actual car. I don't have to walk or bike to work or the grocery store because I have a car. If I didn't have a car I would, in fact, desire one for easy transportation. There would be a spot in my garage completely lacking a car. It would be empty. So the curse is that woman no longer has a perfectly harmonious relationship with man, so she will always have the empty spot. She may have a man but she'll lack the perfect oneness. The perfect bond had been broken and God decreed the woman would be the person forever chasing after it, hoping to reestablish what can never be reestablished at all. That's the consequence and it's not sweet. If you don't believe me on this, watch a few episodes of Dr. Phil or Jerry

Springer or listen to the radio. It won't be long before you realize most relationship problems and pain indeed stem from this empty spot and brokenness we were never designed to have. Watch a few shows, then tell me this isn't a curse—impossible!

So now, not only has sin and discord with God the Giver of Life entered humankind, so have really awful feelings that Adam and Eve had never experienced before. We must assume Adam felt shame because he betrayed Eve, which would likely make him feel defensive, insecure, angry towards himself, and very, very confused. It seems safe to assume Eve felt great hurt, betrayal, fear, aloneness and confusion. Nowhere in Scripture are we told that these feelings were healed. Eve and Adam lived with them the rest of their lives, and their children grew up with them. There was no escaping the feelings so they were passed on and on. Since there was no healing of these painful emotions we were never meant to feel, we've carried them with us generation after generation after generation, unable to free ourselves from them. The difficult, painful feelings haven't gotten any better and we haven't gotten any better at carrying them. Now we're left with the bickering, blaming, and the arguing about underwear or socks on the floor and whose job it was to fill the gas tank. We bring up past hurts, jealousies, and barbs all relationships experience now. We're no longer one with our spouse, but we still have a deep desire for the oneness. We ache to fill the gaping empty spot. We're completely unable to rebuild what once existed and is no more.

So we're left knowing that the best we can do is a good relationship, not a perfect one. Forever on Earth we will experience discord, hurts, and brokenness in all relationships, but that doesn't mean relationships have no value. On the contrary, healthy relationships are vital. We know this because God said it---"It is not good for the man to be alone" (vs. 2:18). So, the best we can do at this point is find a person who's most "suitable" and go from there, problems and all. You've been part of carrying all the brokenness and difficult feelings for generation upon generation, and so has every person you'll ever meet. None of us is even close to perfect anymore, so we're stuck with what we're stuck with---the need for relationship, but also the horrible truth that a perfect relationship can never again exist on Earth because we're completely unable to build and keep one.

Yet we still need thriving, growing relationships, and there are reasonable, healthy things we can do to place ourselves in them.

This book will, hopefully, enlighten you to some positive strengths as well as red flags which may be present in a person and/or a relationship. It will also challenge you to notice things about yourself that might need a little--or a lot--of attention. As you read, take time to ponder each question as it comes up. Passing over a question or idea defeats the purpose of investing your time reading. You don't want to miss anything. A red flag doesn't necessarily mean you terminate a relationship, mind you. It may signal the end, or it might be something to be aware of so that you can consciously and wisely choose to allow the relationship to deepen, being fully aware of the flag-worthy issue. Every relationship will have differences, obstacles, and walls to climb. The essential questions are "How high are those walls?" and "Is this a relationship worth building at all?."

When I was young lo those many years ago, I was taught to be happy any man would have me. (Not exceptional parents, mine.) I was never told that

- I really didn't need a spouse to be complete and
- I was worth far more than to settle for a man blindly
- Just what I should look for in a date, a friend, or a spouse

So I muddled through for decades, making painful mistakes. Hoping to keep my daughters from going through the same pain, I taught, preached, coerced, uplifted, and coached them to the very best of my ability, using wisdom that God brought to my attention. The jury is still out on how much of this wisdom has taken root in my daughters because they're still young, but the guidelines are solid and root-worthy. Because I wish someone had shared these guidelines with me, I'll share them with you. Are they guaranteed to provide you with all skills necessary to be and find the perfect person to enter blissfully into a perfect relationship? Nope, of course not. Complete inability, remember? However, I do promise if you honestly and prayerfully think through even one of the tidbits I offer here you have a far better chance of finding the best—not perfect—relationship. You are likely to be stronger. And therefore all your relationships will be stronger as well.

PART I--BE THE RIGHT PERSON

We assume so often that if we're looking for a relationship of any kind, we just have to get out there and look for somebody—anybody-- and POOF, there's a relationship. We go to singles' groups or bars or join clubs, to meet people, but most of us leave out a big step---making sure we're ready to be in relationship to others. There's a lot of purposeful thinking, planning, and skill-building that is required. Unless that foundation is firmly built, chances are you will falter time and again, never understanding why. So let's first take a look at some very important areas of making sure we are ready for a close relationship.

This may actually be the most challenging but exciting part of the process; getting yourself healthy, honest, and wise enough to be the person God made you to be so that you can have the best, safest, most adventurous and fulfilling relationship that He meant for us all to have in the first place. YOU are the only one that holds the power to be ready for your relationship. If you don't at least consider making some changes in your level of awareness, your behavior, your perspective, and presentation you'll probably have the same disappointing, hurtful relationships that you've had before. Since you're investing the time to read this book, I assume that isn't what you want, so take a deep breath and PLUNGE.

CHAPTER 1-- BE A PERSON WHO'S HONEST ABOUT WHO THEY ARE

This is the time for brutal, blunt honesty with yourself. Remember, nothing changes unless you face it bravely. You might be thinking "Oh, great, she's going to say "'face your weaknesses.'" Gee, I've never heard THAT before" and there might be an accompanying eye roll. But WAIT! Don't put aside this book and reach for the remote or even yawn. Keep reading a few pages and you might find something different from what you expected.

It seems to me that it's exceedingly hard for most people, Christians in particular, in American society to acknowledge and proudly display our great attributes, of which we all have many. Humans were created by the breath of God—surely anything that has even a tiny fraction of God-breath has wondrousness beyond measure! The fact is, though, in many cases, both men and women find it difficult—even shameful—to seriously CELEBRATE OURSELVES and who we're created to be. Does this come from our parents or grandparents telling us it isn't nice to brag? I don't know, and I don't care because it really doesn't matter. It simply is what we've been conditioned to do. We say things like "Oh, thanks for the compliment but I'm sure you could've done it better" or "Oh, I just got lucky on that" or "Don't thank me, thank God" when we've accomplished or been something delight-worthy. Notice when a co-worker or friend gives or receives a compliment....nine times out of ten the receiver downplays their accomplishment and hurriedly changes the subject. Most likely you'll even see them dip their head for a second, as if they feel ashamed they're so unworthy of praise.

When we hang our heads and act like our efforts and accomplishments aren't worth much, this isn't humility. It isn't God-honoring. We may mean for it to be humility, we may intend for it to at least seem like humility but it's really a lie. And where do lies come from? We have an enemy who is "The father of all lies" (John 8:44) and who takes great glee in our shame because it keeps us removed from the joyous, appreciative relationship with our Daddy Creator since we feel so unworthy and dirty-rags-ish (Isaiah 64:6) that we cannot conceive of a God who wants us to come close to Him.

Stop this right now! Yes, only God has given you your strengths, talents, and abilities and yes, you can do nothing without His guidance, but to shrug off your awesomeness is to deny God's glorious, miraculous presence in your life and how AMAZING His image is; the same image in which we are created. Our wonderful Creator WANTS us to be aware and proud of what He's made you to be.

We've probably all heard the Scripture saying He knit us before we were born. I'm not a knitter but I imagine it's a long process to turn out a nice creation. The knitter has to intentionally choose the pattern, purchase just the right yarn, and find the time and concentration to painstakingly form the desired outcome. They interlock all the necessary steps and colors, until the knitter finally creates something they're pleased with and want to show off to their friends and family. God has done exactly this for you. He has CHOSEN each of us, PURCHASED us, INVESTED TIME in us and TOOK unimaginable PAINS to interlock our beings in exactly the way He intended. Surely He wants to show us off! Why wouldn't He? He's proud of what He has made and wants the world to know what He's done! Some versions of the Bible actually refer to us as God's MASTERPIECES (Eph. 2:10). It's not possible that God, after making each one of us, says "Yeah, he's okay, but I wish I'd made him thinner" or "Oh, thanks, Gabriel. Yeah, I like how she turned out, but I bet you could've done better." No way!! Our Creator joyfully gives us just the wonderful characteristics of His that He wants to showcase in us! Thank Him for how He made you, and acknowledge boldly and cheerfully the talents, skills, and uniqueness He gave you.

So now we are coming to the "brutal honesty" part. You must become aware of what's great about you and not-so-much so you can position yourself to build good relationships. There is possible pain and risk involved in your awareness. We'll talk in more depth in later chapters about your weaknesses and what to do about them and how to get on the challenging and sometimes sad and scary paths to strengthen these areas, but you must also be willing to acknowledge your glorious strengths. This can sometimes feel much riskier and terrifying.

"How can looking at my strengths be terrifying?" you might ask. It's because if you acknowledge your vast potential and live it you can no longer hide behind the false "humility" you built about yourself that protects you from failing. To live in your strengths means you reveal them to yourself and to the world. This can be blood-freezingly terrifying. For instance, I have a LOT to say about the whole Right Person/Right Relationship thing (obviously, and much to my daughters' eye rolling dismay) and I have a couple small writing accomplishments of which I'm proud, so I should feel fairly confident in writing this book but nope, I don't. I. Am. TERRIFIED of submitting my finished book to an editor or publisher because if it's rejected that will prove to the universe that I am in fact worthless and that nothing I contribute to the world could ever possibly have value. I struggle against the thought of just putting down my laptop and forgetting the whole thing. If I put my best work out there, I'll be laughed at, rejected and humiliated, so it's probably better that I hide.

This is extreme, irrational, and untrue of course, but don't we all experience similar terror? Probably you feel that if you live 100 percent full-out you may stumble and fall and believe you've irrevocably failed and are proven worthless? All of us feel that fear, at least from time to time. So we hang back, look away when there's proof of our God-created greatness in front of us, and shrink back further into the "humility" that keeps us from brilliantly shining His glory. It's easier. Shrinking back and not showing our gifts and talents demands less of us, requires less risk. Easier, but it doesn't point to the wondrousness that could have only been placed in us by a Creator full of creativity and glee and love.

To BE the right person to enter into a relationship you MUST be 100 percent willing to admit that in some areas you're broken, or at least chipped, but you also MUST be 100 percent willing to acknowledge in other areas you are GREAT. You must be certain you were created with marvelous attributes and talents that make you incredibly capable and gifted when it comes to accomplishing certain things, and you are VALUABLE. Are you willing to shrug off the fake humility, get out of God's way, and let Him radiate through you? Do it! You're able to radiate so much of Him!

CHAPTER 2-- BE A PERSON WHO'S AWARE OF WHO THEY ARE

So, who the heck are you? What are your strengths? What are your "chips" or weaknesses? Many people find it much easier to rattle off their weaknesses than to list even one strength. Let's start you're your positives; go ahead and list as many as you can think of, using the space on the next page. Feel free to ask God to show you the wonderful qualities He gave you. Don't rush—linger and ponder. Think of your appearance, habits, inner traits, how you treat people, skills you have learned, strengths you possess that have helped you get through dark times, etc. Think about what your friends or family compliment you about, or request from you. Don't feel like you're bragging—if you're good at something or have a great characteristic, list it. You make your list, I'll wait for you.

Okay, good job. If you have less than ten items on your list, though, go back to it. If it was easy coming up with ten, think of five more and maybe go a little deeper. I'll finish my tea.

As you look at your list of at least ten positive attributes, are you sitting up a little taller? Are you a little more pleased with Lake YOU? Remember this is a time to celebrate the God-given greatness of you, so enjoy your list. Add to it generously, as new thoughts occur to you.

Now let's go to your weak areas. List them as well. Use the page provided, so you can easily compare your notes on both lists. Take all the time you need to ponder and don't be afraid to put it all on paper. Not writing them down doesn't mean they don't exist and impede you. Don't lie to yourself. If you have a trait you don't like or is unacceptable, list it. Again, ask your Maker to show you those weak areas. He knows them and wants to help you with them. Psalm 139:24 shows us David asking God to "see if there be any hurtful way in me, and lead me in the everlasting way."

Don't list every mistake you ever made. Instead, list out why you made the mistake. Were you too gullible, too angry, not cautious enough, or ....? This is a listing of traits, habits and beliefs that require a good look-see, to see if a) they are true and b) how you can best work around them.

You see, we've all been told negative things about ourselves that are untrue but we still believe them. You need to shed these untruths. You are striving here for brutal honesty, remember. For example, if you never agreed with your mother when she told you you're clumsy, don't list it! If, however, you know she was correct in her assessment and you have always had difficulty walking across a room without hearing a thud or a crash behind you, then list it. It's fine. It's okay if you happen to be clumsy; it's part of who you are, so put it on your list. Don't be shy about your list of negatives or weak areas. It's not like adding something to your list risks someone seeing the list and finding out about your less-than-perfectness. People know your weaknesses (and strengths) and your lists won't surprises to them. Even if someone does audaciously read your personal list and sees something that surprises them, who cares? Your assessment of who you are is your assessment No one else gets to approve it. Listen to your own voice, and the still, small voice of the One who created you.

LIST OF MY POSITIVES

LIST OF MY WEAK AREAS

In May of 2003 I heard this voice clear and loud which led to my friends' favorite "Jill Story." I was driving along one day listening to Christian radio and I asked God to specifically show me why He loved me. I knew He does, I just didn't know why He loved me so personally and deeply. So within a couple days I got an answer. I was minding my own business taking my older daughter to the library. I decided to head first to our mailbox cluster on the corner of our little street about four houses away. Just before the turn to the cluster, we came upon a very earth-stopping and eerily weird sight: an elderly man was laying on the front yard of a neighbor's home. Now, we live in Phoenix, Arizona—laying in the yard does NOT mean he was in the cool grass relaxing and looking at cloud formations. No, he was laying on thousands of palm-sized or smaller ROCKS. In the late afternoon heat on a 105 degree day! Lord! He didn't look good, and I had a feeling I cannot describe of just knowing he was no longer in this world. This certainly wasn't something I ever planned for, but I knew that some action was called for since I was the only...well, living....adult on the scene and my daughter was watching me. How to role model THIS? I hopped out of the car, then noticed a pool maintenance guy ringing the doorbell of a house about three houses farther down the street. Hoping I could slough this situation off to someone else I called out, squeakily, "Um, excuse me sir. Sir? Is he with you? Maybe your dad or something?" and pointed down to the rocks where the man was laying. From the angle the pool man was standing he had no idea what I was talking about until his eyes followed my pointing finger.

I'll never forget that man slowly looking back up at me with a horrified expression that clearly said "Lady, why in God's name would I leave my DAD collapsed on ROCKS in this HEAT, while calmly ringing a doorbell??" Good unspoken point, sir. So, although I have been certified in CPR multiple times, I leaned over and did what came to mind---I gingerly reached out my little finger and squeaked out, "Sir? Sir? Are you all right?" What exactly did I think my little finger barely touching his by-now-hot arm was going to do? And how did I think he could possibly answer me? I knew he was beyond the point of sitting up, rubbing his eyes and saying he must've nodded off! Or, how did I think it was helping when I answered the 911 Dispatcher's question about our location by saying "Oh, uh, I'm just on the corner by my mailbox?"

Much later, once I had collected my thoughts I realized this story, meaning absolutely no disrespect to the deceased neighbor (whose name, we later were told was, ironically, Ed. We now call that whole situation the Dead Ed Episode) was God's answer to my question of why He loves me in particular—I crack Him up! Of course, the death of Ed is not a funny situation and I am sure that God was in no way laughing at that. Death is never funny. But, He knew that Ed was going to pass away that day, and He decided to put me on the scene to do.....whatever I would do. I got sort of a vision or a sense of Him calling some angels over saying, "Okay, watch what she's going to do. Watch her try to help but really be a goof-ball! She's so funny!" I think He might've rolled with laughter when I had to tell the mother of my younger daughter's friend who was visiting us that afternoon that six year old Maddie had unfortunately seen a dead body. The mom's shocked response was

"Oh, God—did you go to South Phoenix?" My chagrined answer was "No, we went to our mailbox."

Hopefully you can see the dark humor in the story but I also hope you see the truth that came to me: I am loved just because He made me, despite my occasional ding-bat, silly, less than useful actions. I was mortified by my ineptness but my heart sings to this day with the knowledge that my Creator finds amusement watching me! And, He cared enough to give me an answer to my question! Some of the negative things I grew up hearing might, in times of high and eerie stress, actually be true, but it's okay as long as I know it, admit it, and try to work around it.

We all must navigate around our weak areas because we all have some. We just do. If God made us all perfect in every way we would be exactly the same and that would be no fun whatsoever! For instance, humanity needs reckless people so we can have adventures, and we need serious, no nonsense people so we can have medical treatments, space exploration or whatever brainy things they come up with, and we need people who don't constantly dwell in common sense and practicality so we can have art, whimsy and purple pirate-themed birthday parties for kids.

But how do you turn the recklessness, the overly-seriousness or the ding-bat-ness or whatever other "negative" item on your list into something you can live with? The answer is simple— if it's not something that can be changed through life-coaching or counseling you must accept it and move boldly forth. Look at it with a different mirror, probably from different angles. If you listed "I'm horrible at math" as a weakness, accept it as truth but also look at what your brain is adept at. While your brain's left side might not be the one that primarily drives you, your right side kicks in with lots of useful items. Perhaps you're good with language or creativity or you're intuitive. Sometimes a negative is simply a bad habit that can easily be changed. Other times a negative is just a darn negative. List it, acknowledge it and make peace with it. Sometimes a different perspective is called for when we honestly appraise ourselves. If you're not able to gain a more workable perspective on your weak areas by yourself, this might be a very good time to talk with a counselor or life coach who can help you see that your biggest negative isn't something you should hang your head and walk in shame about for the rest of your life. Our traits do NOT determine our worth. Ever.

Your worth is not dependent on how you feel about yourself or if you have more positive traits than negative traits listed, thank God. Literally, thank God for this—He declares us His most valuable creation over and over daily without regard to our moods, what the mean neighbor next door said about our yard, if we are having a bad hair day, if we are divorced or single, if we slept well last night, or any of the endless possibilities. Let's be very clear here—these lists you've created listing your positive qualities and weaker qualities are not to be used as a scale to determine if you are a valuable person or not. They are a tool to help you clearly see the 'package' that is you, so that you can move forward in your quest to BE the right person in your relationships.

All righty, are you finished with your list? I hope you didn't list more than 18 or 20 items on the list—no one is that awful! If you did, take a few moments to trim your list back to 15 or so items.

Okay, now put the two lists together in a way that's clear and helpful to you. It may be helpful to draw an outline of a person to represent you and write all the items from both lists inside the outline. This will give you a clearer picture of yourself. If you can lie on the floor or stand against the wall on a large piece of paper like packaging paper or newsprint paper and have someone safely and respectfully draw an actual outline of you, all the better! This will make the resulting outline more personal. Don't draw features or detailed clothing or-- for the love of Pete-- details in body parts. This is a place for word lists to be seen without interference.

So, what do you see? Is your outline a pretty accurate picture of you? Do you need to add or erase anything? Did you learn anything about yourself, or did this exercise confirm the self assessment you already had? If you have a friend or loved one who is safe and very honest, let them look at your outline. Do they have constructive feedback for you? Is there anything they would add or remove from the list? Don't make changes in your list or outline just because someone else says to, but spend some time evaluating honest feedback.

If your outline seems pretty accurate, decide how you feel about the entire picture. Take a few moments now to think through the questions below; they're crucial to the goal of Being you want to BE to find your great relationship.

- Is this who you want to be?
- Do any of the traits listed bring out strong emotions in you, like pride, sadness, or embarrassment or joy?
- Do you like the person depicted on this list and believe others can and should like you, too?
- If this wasn't a picture of you, how would you feel about this person? If someone else held these traits, both the strong areas and the weak ones, would you think highly of them?
- Does any part of this person you've outlined come off the paper screaming at you to "FIX ME!"?

The next few chapters may help you build up and transform any of the less-liked and less-healthy traits on the list you just worked so hard to create. We can surely figure out ways to quiet all that screaming!

CHAPTER 3-- BE A PERSON WHO PRESENTS THEIR BEST TO THE WORLD

Now that you have a strong awareness of who you are it's time to figure out how you want to help others see you accurately so you can form healthy relationships. Presenting yourself in a positive and genuine light to the people you come in contact with takes a lot of honest self-appraising thought, planning and practice to do it right. More brutal honesty is required.

When you walk into a roomful of people you've never yet met before, what do you tell them about yourself before you even speak? What do you want them to see? For example, do they see a person who

- cares about their appearance
- respects others by dressing for the occasion
- walks confidently
- seems friendly with good eye contact and a cheerful facial expression

Or do they see a hesitant, shy person who's uncomfortable being where they are ? Or maybe they see even a bored, arrogant jerk? Your answer to this question lead to the next question—is that what you WANT people to see and think of you? First impressions can become a long-term one, so it is critical you effectively communicate who you are right from the start. Take a moment to write down, in one sentence only, who you want the roomful of strangers to see when they see you for the first time. What is your goal for how you initially present yourself? Here are several ideas, to help you formulate your own Goal Statement:

"When they look at me,

I want people to see a ___________________"

Confident, smart, God-driven, vibrant, capable, younger-looking-than-I-am woman who's a safe, fun person to be around and has a lot to offer (This one is my goal, and it took me a few minutes to formulate, actually! I'm glad I did—I have a couple adjustments to make!)

- Gentle, kind, artistic man who reflects Christ as best he can
- Very important person who's always moving toward bigger and better things

- A wise, creative, fun young woman who loves God and her family and is accomplishing great thing

Take a few hours or even days to sit with this goal until it feels right for you. Does it fit you? Do you believe it's in line with who God created you to be? Ask your friends and family if they think it fits you. How close do they see you to being the person you want to be? Write down your thoughts and their feedback so you can review it from time to time.

Your Goal Statement must be reasonable and attainable. For example, you cannot have a goal of being seen as a musically gifted, sought-after dynamic performer if you have never learned to read music or play an instrument and are pants-wetting terrified of being on a stage and therefore have never done so. Nor is it realistic to hope to present yourself as a glamorous super-model type when you haven't washed your hair since two Thursdays ago and you tripped over your toenails as you came into the room. Likewise, it's unlikely you'll be seen as a fun-loving, carefree life-of-the-party if you've done nothing but scowl and stand alone against the wall since you came into the room. Those are attainable goals, mind you, but they must be true and what you show to the world. You can't fool people into thinking you're something you obviously aren't, so don't even try it. You'll just come off as a phony, and no one finds that appealing. Falseness won't get you the relationship(s) you want.

GOAL STATEMENT

Chances are you didn't write down a goal statement that says you hope people see you as a dowdy, uncool, uncoordinated boob or as an unkempt, smelly loser. You didn't write that, did you? If you did, you probably need another book before you're ready for this one. So, assuming you want to present yourself in a positive way to a roomful of strangers or to the blind date that you've been looking forward to, or to your friend/co-worker of 20 years, let's take a close and honest look at your presentation.

Appearance

You knew this would be the first look-see, didn't you? Yes, yes, I know... it's soooo judgemental to measure people by their outer appearance such as clothes, hair dye color, facial expression, etc. but guess what? WE ALL DO IT ALL THE TIME. You know it's true, so let's not get bogged down in the "its not okay to judge based on looks" stuff. Stop sputtering and rolling your eyes and telling me that it's 2021 and I shouldn't be shallow. Yes, yes, one's heart is more important to God. No doubt about that. 1 Samuel 16:7 is the well-known verse that says people look at the outward appearance, but the Lord looks at the heart. He can, but humans are limited and we can only see the outside, at least initially. That's why our appearance—how we choose to express ourselves to the world—is very important to BEing the right person who will FIND the right person. Everyone sizes up everyone else based on their outward appearance because that's all that we have at the first moment to form an opinion and decide whether a person is safe and approachable or if something about them sends up a red flag telling us to be careful. It's part of our survival instinct to do so. Your appearance is your first introduction to those we meet, and it matters. It's not judgmental or shallow to believe this; it's wise and realistic.

So, let's go at it:

- How clean are you? I mean, how pleasant are you to be around? If you were crossing a street walking alongside a stranger would they quicken their step so as not to be confused with someone who's actually with you? Seriously, is your hair matted, or neatly styled and clean? How are your fingernails? Yesterday's yard work or last week's paint job shouldn't be caked under your nails. Do you need dental care because your smile shows neglected, uncared-for teeth?

- Do your clothes fit? Were they recently laundered and hopefully purchased this century? (Yikes--This is one I need to attend to—some of the things in my closet are older than my adult children and they are NOT coming back into style. I have to face that, throw out some things, and move on.) Do your clothes reflect your goal statement? For instance, I have vowed to never ever buy another scoop-necked, rounded top because I look OLD in them. Old and frumpy, like the nosy neighbor lady who's a side character in a Hallmark® movie. Maybe there's nothing wrong with being a neighbor lady in a Hallmark® movie but it doesn't fit my goal statement. If I'm dressing like the nosy lady I'm not looking younger than my real age, probably not sharply smart, and what I have to offer may look quite questionable. If your goal statement says you want to look like an intelligent, valuable businesswoman but your clothes are skimpy tube-tops, skin-tight leather mini-skirts and hooker shoes and you wear more make-up than Mimi on the Drew Carey Show, that probably does not add up. (If you're not familiar with Mimi, Google her. Scary.)

What IS the look you want, and how can you go about getting it from your clothes? Is your 'look' still in vogue? Are your skinny jeans still 'in'? (I am really asking this---I don't know if skinny jeans are still ok to wear, but I need to find out asap because I have some in my closet that I wear!) Is it still (was it really ever?) cool and tough-looking to have your lovely hind-end showing because your pants were hanging well below it, guys? Flesh belts are not a consistent look if you want to be seen as professional and trustworthy. It's a smart idea to periodically peruse our closets and drawers and purge what no longer truly gives you the look you wanted when you bought it. This is a painful necessity I need to do. Um, I'll be back in a couple of hours.....

Ok, I'm back, and my closet is purged. Now that my immediate closet wardrobe needs are met, let's continue....

- Ladies, do you dress like the valuable person you are? Don't present yourself as if you're cheap. People are eager to avoid "paying" more than what something seems worth. If a person presents themselves cheaply, they won't attract people who are willing to "pay" attention, respect, or time, for them.
- Women understand that men are usually visual beings. Men are generally attracted by what they see as opposed to having an emotional attraction and women often dress accordingly when trying to attract a man. Since men are also sexual beings, women often confuse the need to dress attractively with the idea they should show off all their sexual assets. This is a fatal error. It just looks cheap. Men can often get signals that are different than what you intended, so don't make it easy for them to misjudge your value. They ain't called "hooker shoes" for no reason. Beloved actress Betty

White, on the TV show Hot in Cleveland, occasionally told the three young women who shared her home, "You look like hookers!" when they were dressed to go on a date or to a bar (well, her character did. I doubt that Betty actually told Valerie Bertinelli, Jane Leeves or Wendi Malick this). She thought they were showing too much skin and looked way too ready-for-sex-at-any-cost. It was adorably blunt, as only Betty White can pull off. The truth is, the characters often DID look like they might be of questionable vocation because of how short their dresses were, or how low their necklines were, or how high their heels were. They dressed, as women so often do, as if they had no confidence in their appearance unless they catered to a man's presumed need to be hit over the head with their sexuality. They were all beautiful, gorgeous, enviable women who looked great anytime and didn't need to show more cleavage than normal or wear tighter skirts just to get the attention of the men in the room. Do you understand why??

Because dressing in a sexually provocative way only draws a man's attention to the sex aspect of a woman. It clobbers him over the head with too much boobs, butt and legs, and it skips him right past the lovely smile, the natural eye sparkle, or the delightful sense of humor. When a woman does this she is communicating "I am only one dimensional, only able to offer one thing, and I'm not worth much because this one thing is all I've got." Well, guess what... a person who presents themselves as cheap or of not much value is going to attract those who do not want to invest much in them. If I present myself cheaply, why would anyone invest much time, attention, effort, or energy, into me? I've already told them I'm not worth that. Of course you should wear a flattering dress or a cute top, but make sure it communicates "My appearance is only one great part of who I am, it's not the only part! I'm worth much more than just a quickie."

- I am in no way suggesting that we women must dress as perpetual frumps in baggy clothes and dowdy, drab colors! Of course not! Present yourself as attractively as possible but avoid giving the message of easy sexual availability. If you don't believe me, try it a few times I think you will get a much different response than you are used to getting if you dial down the sex focus.

- Men, how are you lookin' these days? Do your clothing choices appeal to a person with the qualities you want in those around you? If your clothing shouts "Look at me—I'm rich and successful" it may also communicate "I want someone who is only interested in my performance, income, and success, not me." This means you cannot complain about the shallowness of your relationships because you have landed the "fish" that you baited your hook to catch. Or do your clothes scream "I'm sloppy and unkempt because I can't take care of my own ironing and laundry. I need help taking care of myself," you may be communicating that you need a caretaker rather than a close adult relationship. If you look like a teenage boy who has never seen a washing machine, you give up the right to complain that your relationships seem to be with mothering, care-taking women who treat you like a child. Dress as attractively as possible making sure that sloppy clothing isn't what people see first. Keep your pants pulled up (PLEASE!) and shirts tucked or untucked appropriately, no chili stains on the t-shirts, and leave behind the expensive suits that give off the message you're just a little better than everyone else.

- Make sure how you dress reflects that your appearance may be the first great thing about you people notice but by no means is it the only one. Dress in a way that invites people to approach you, to discover all your wonderful traits.
- How do you smell, honestly? Obviously body odor is a big no-no, but any smell that invades others' space probably won't work for you. Even the most expensive cologne or aftershave should NOT result in others backing away from

you with their eyes tearing up and their noses running. Several years ago I had a boss of a boss who made her presence known before she even entered the room, and not in a good way. Her strong perfume-cloud arrived long before she did and, frankly, made me dislike her at our first introduction. It was offensive to me that she had no awareness or concern that people around her might be sensitive to strong smells or just didn't care for hers. She had no right to presume everyone wanted to smell her favorite perfume the rest of the day even when she left at noon. Because of my sensitivity to such strong scents I had to make it a point to stay far from her and others in our company did the same thing. It was probably not the reaction she intended every morning as she filled her tub with her perfume and rolled around in it in the morning or whatever the heck she did. Presumably she was trying to enhance her general presentation. She failed. Epic.

- While we're discussing smells, it should be a law that mints are mandatory after drinking a cup of coffee. Is there anything worse than coffee breath a couple hours after the fresh brew was enjoyed? Unfortunately, bad breath may be an issue without our having any awareness, so being in the habit of popping a breath mint throughout the day is probably a good one. You may not be able to catch every bad breath moment but hopefully you can avoid getting a reputation for being foul-mouthed in an odiferous way.

- What about tats and piercings and unnatural hair dyes? Excessive piercings and pink or green hair may be okay for kids, but do they reflect the respectable adult you want to be seen as? Does the nose ring permanently dangling from your nose really say "Yes! I'm ready for restaurant leadership at a high corporate level"? Does your pinkish purple hair really convince others that you are fun and free-spirited at age 45, or does it just make you look confused or ridiculous? Are your tats beautiful art most people would appreciate? Do you hide behind tats, piercings or outlandish hair color, hoping attention will be drawn to the outlandish aspect and not on you? These are excellent questions to ask your honest and safe friends, or maybe it's time for a heart-to-heart with your own mirror. A full-length one. Maybe your tats, piercings and "creative" hair color absolutely match your goal statement. If so, great! Good job! But if not, you need to acknowledge that and adjust accordingly. "Death to All Authority" tattoos with weapons and blood droplets probably won't go over well in a job interview.

- What about your weight? Does your body size reflect the health you want others to see? If you want to be seen as a fit, active person who respects yourself enough to take care of your body, you cannot be 40 pounds underweight and look emaciated or be so overweight you waddle, have to pause twice and breathe heavily just walking from your car to the grocery store doorway where you will fight middle-schoolers for the scooters with baskets. This is a time for the brutal honesty; while an extra 10 or 15 pounds most of us can't shake might not be a big deal, an extra 100 or 200 probably is a problem. Similarly, thinness to the point of looking like you'll snap into 8 pieces if you're hugged might not be your ideal presentation. Remember, your goal is to invite people closer, not hide behind extra weight or a fragile-looking body. Right or wrong, an unhealthy-looking body weight can make others veer away from you because they may assume you have emotional or physical issues they simply don't want to deal with in a close relationship. Get feedback from your doctor about what a healthy weight for you is, and go once again to your safe friends or family members to see how close they think you come to that healthy weight. Make a strong effort to get to a healthy weight and wear your weight confidently, whatever it is.

- Whatever your size or height, wear it proudly! If you're a tall woman, stand tall! Put your shoulders back, lift your head, wear your high heels! Ditto for whether you're thin, heavy, short, or whatever. Remember confidence is revealed by good posture, a friendly smile and good eye contact, and confidence is a great pull.

OTHER ASPECTS OF YOUR PRESENTATION

Okay, now we've covered the basics as far as first-sights and first-smells are concerned. Now it's time to go a little deeper.

- What does your facial expression say about you? Are you friendly, approachable or kind of scary? A popular phrase now is "resting face." What does your face communicate to others when you're not 'on'? It's easy to give a wrong impression with an unintentional, unbeknownst-to-yourself scowl. Try to monitor your expressions by being more consciously aware of them. When you walk through a park, an office hallway or through your neighborhood alone, take a moment to think of what others see on your face as they pass by. What do you want people to see on your face? If you want to look like you're praying without ceasing or thinking intently about finding a solution to a problem or looking for new friends along the way, adjust your face accordingly.

- We all know body language is crucially important and that most communication is non-verbal, so what are you doing with this? When you enter the room, how do you carry yourself? Do you shuffle in or barge in scowling, or do you enter poised with a steady pace and a friendly expression? Does the way you carry yourself announce that you respect yourself and others, and you expect it in return? Pay attention to your posture. It is as important as what your grandmother told you! Can you walk well in the shoes you are wearing? We have all seen women in heels so high they walk like a giraffe that's just had a painful pedicure! Or their body pitches forward unattractively like a marionette with an inexperienced marionnettiste (This is a real word. I looked it up!). Not a good look for you, the poor giraffe or the puppet master. Whatever your goal statement is and whatever you chose to wear or sport, OWN that. Be in control of and confident about what you chose, or the look is just silly and not authentic, like a kid pretending to be a grownup. Practice paying attention to how your body is positioned when you walk. Is your posture what you want it to be? Are your eyes looking at where you want to directed them? And what about your arms? Are they crossed, giving off an air of defensiveness? Is your chin up, saying "I dare ya to mess with me?" Are your shoulders slouched or back nicely?

I personally believe the most important thing about our non-verbal communication is how we hold our heads. Yep, our heads. For the love of Pete, people, LIFT UP YOUR HEADS! A bowed head screams of shame, a lack of confidence, a lack of belief in self-worth, and it invites victimization! Shame isn't appealing. Confidence looks much better and draws people in. A lifted head gives the message, "I can take on the world," and "I know that I won't trip over my own feet." There's NO PLACE for a bowed head or slumped shoulders in a Christian's presentation. Psalm 3:3 says God actually lifts up our heads—let's not put them back down! No matter what bad parents have said for the first 18+ of our lives or our spouse said yesterday or (shuddering) what our teenagers tell their friends about us when they know we can hear them and they are mad at us, we have NO reason to live in shame and to project otherwise in our presentation to the world is ......well, shameful because we, as followers of Jesus, KNOW how valuable we are don't we, and how much we cost Him? He thinks we're worthy of leaving beautiful Heaven and coming down to rainy, cold, dirty Earth and dying for us so He gets to live in our hearts, not shame! Never minimize this fact, or indicate "Yeah, Jesus did that, but it wasn't enough to make ME worthwhile." Make the choice to move away from that lie right out of Hell!

It is likely that you (and everyone else) will in fact do things in life that earn you—or should earn you—shame, embarrassment or even mortification for a short time, but you do not have to live in those moments! It's impossible for you to be healthy enough for a close, positive relationship if you believe you should be ashamed of your very self, especially if you're quick to communicate that to others. So, gol-durn it, lift up that head and communicate to everyone every time that YOU are proud of who you were created to be, and you're thankful to God for making you so extraordinary! Not too high, mind you—the goal isn't to look down one's nose at everyone, but to make sure you're not staring at your feet or examining your navel because you live your life weighed down by feelings of inadequacy.

One of my favorite sayings comes from speaker and author Liz Curtis Higgs. She says, "It's hard to see God when you are looking down." She is so right---all we can see when we look down and live with a bowed head is our own feet. Not even anyone else's feet, just ours. How boring, pointless and lonely. There's so much more your Creator wants you to see. Look UP. Even from your cell phone! What you see endlessly on your social network feed is nowhere near as important or glorious as what God has for you to see. LOOK UP!!

- Hand-in-hand with keeping your head up is to maintain good eye contact with people. Most likely your goal statement requires you to be in the habit of making eye contact regularly with people. This is so hard to do at times, isn't it? Sometimes I just don't wanna look someone in the eye because I don't want them to see a secret I 'm holding or maybe (hard swallow) to see my real feelings toward them. I want my eyes to be clear and my whole body full of light like it says in Matthew 6:22 but sometimes I don't feel all sweetness and light. Certainly you don't want to always have a piercing, unrelenting stare at someone because that is flippin' freaky, but a nice flow of relaxed and interested eye-to-eye contact can make you appear more trustworthy, attentive, and attractive. If this is an area you're uncomfortable in, you need to build up this skill. Think about what would be a good way to practice, such as using your mirror, or practicing on a friend or family member, or even committing to counting to three while holding eye contact with someone, for starters. You'll be amazed at how quickly it becomes easier!

- What is your voice like? Is it pleasant in tone and volume or too soft and hard to hear or loud or grating? You can't be shocked or upset if you're overlooked in a crowd when someone must shush everyone in the room and turn down the music to hear your answer to "How are you?" because you didn't put the effort into having a voice that is strong and confident. Or, do people back away from you, grimacing as the walls shake when you boom out "GREAT"? Do you get feedback your accent is strong and difficult to understand? People don't like to look stupid or awkward and often won't talk to someone that they cannot understand and must keep asking for repetition of words or phrases. If it just takes too much effort to figure out if you're saying "Good morning" or "Timmy just fell into a well!" people are likely to avoid conversing with you. Is this fair and kind? Probably not, but it is what it is. Pay attention to what happens when you speak and make a log for a day or two of the reaction you get. If you see a problematic pattern, notice it and adjust accordingly.

- What is the content of your speech? Check yourself for self-absorbed conversation, or speech riddled with words people don't want to hear like obscenities (no, dropping the f-bomb does not make you sound cool or intelligent. It makes you appear common and ignorant, with no substance to what you are saying. Stop it.), slurs of any kind, negativity, or even the dreaded know-it-all content. These do not help you, they hurt you. Again, pay attention to what happens when you speak; do people tend to enjoy chatting with you, or do they fall away quickly? Do you leave voicemails that typically go unreturned? Notice what happens if you're interrupted while telling a story or sharing your opinion. Does the listener want you to continue after the distracting incident has passed, or do they go on to another topic?

- I once worked with a young woman who was.....well, boring! She had a sad-sack personality, always talking about how pitiful her life was, even though it really wasn't, and she had full control over the sort-of-pitiful parts but she simply chose to complain instead of making changes. She seemed to have absolutely nothing of any worth or interest to say. She didn't comment on current events, ask about the other person's life, discuss TV shows or movies, or talk about interesting people she knew. There was nothing anyone could latch on to and engage in conversation with her. In fact, one time we passed in the hallway and, seeing the pink top I was wearing, she exclaimed-and I do mean exclaimed—this was exciting to her- "I wore pink YESTERDAY!" What could I say to THAT? Replying with, "Yes! The color pink was just discovered and I dared to wear it" didn't seem sincere or kind. I honestly tried to think of where to take that convo, but nothing came to me (still hasn't!) so I gave some lame response and walked on to the restroom. I avoided her in the future as much as possible because I didn't want to deal with the awkwardness. This probably wasn't the most kind or mature response, but I had no idea how to build on nothing. If you want to build a healthy relationship, you have to learn to converse in a way that engages others!

While we're on the subject of appearance and presentation, do you appear when you're supposed to? Are you punctual? This speaks volumes about your time management skills, your motivation and your respect for others' time and schedule.

- Finally, how is your handshake? This is extremely difficult to master, because how do we know? We cannot shake hands with ourselves. It's the wrong angle, even if we try. (Oh, uh, not that I have. That'd be dorky.) How can you tell if you have the dreaded cold, limp fish or the crushing shake? I honestly don't know what to tell you about this one. Perhaps you could have a few friends over for 'shakes' but not the thick creamy kind you need a straw for but to practice handshaking. Be aware of how you do it—and the reaction you get—on this odd but almost constant part of our culture.

At this point you've either a) taken notes and made some adjustments to your appearance or b) confirmed for yourself that you're on top of these issues and need no further help in this area. Whichever it is, be proud of yourself for making the most of what God has given you! Stand tall! And lift your head!

CHAPTER 4-- BE A PERSON WHO HAS THEIR 'BAGGAGE' UNPACKED AND UNDER CONTROL

"Let all bitterness and wrath and anger and clamor and slander be put away from you, along with malice." Ephesians 4: 31, English Standard Version Bible.

This, my wonderful reading friends, is baggage. We all have it, and it gets in the way of having healthy and thriving relationships. Everyone has baggage because we've all been crushed, disrespected, overlooked, invisible, abused and made to feel like worm poo at some times in our lives. Some people more than others, but no one gets out unscarred. It hurts so much.

We were not designed to hold such pain and hurt. We were designed to frolic in perfect fellowship with each other and our Creator who made such a wondrous place for us to do so. But Adam Eve messed that up and so began the lies, betrayal, disrespect, bruising and irreparable wounding --even killing-- of hearts and bodies. Because we were never meant to hold such things, we have had to make our own holding places for the feelings we're stuck with. So, we gather these horrors together, look at them from every painful angle and then put them as far away from our conscious functioning as we possibly can. We lock them up, or at least try to. We don't know how to end what we were never meant to carry so instead of having past wounds and past traumas we keep them alive. They quickly compost into bitterness, wrath, anger, clamor, lies to ourselves and others and finally the big ugly "M" word—malice. Ugly indeed, but of course we harbor this in our hearts. What else could we do with it all?

Putting the hurts, threats, lies, and all the rest into bags seems like a good idea at the time, but sooner or later they break and spill. Always. Out spill the malice, slander, wrath, clamor, and anger. Sometimes we direct it at others and the result is sarcasm, unkindness, passive/aggressiveness, control, etc. Sometimes we direct it at ourselves and the result is unearned guilt, shame, depression, anxiety, and other negative emotions.. No matter how we direct it it isn't good. That's why God wants us to get rid of it.

Sometimes what's spilled out is pretty easily cleaned up. An honest look at an incident might lead you to understand that the hurt flung at you was really about the other person and had nothing to do with you at all, so you can toss that item out for good—no need to re-stuff it. A good example of this is the one-finger salute you got while driving because you didn't slam on your brakes to let someone cut in front of you. That's all about the saluter, not you, the salutee. Another person's rudeness doesn't mean you're a horrible driver and there's no reason to hang your head over this incident. The saluter is allowing his baggage to control his actions and the spill splashed on you. It's not about you, so dismiss any incriminating thoughts you had about your driving skills. This isn't your baggage. Don't let anyone else put their junk in your bags.

However often what spills out of our baggage is more harmful to us and our relationships and is not so easily cleaned up. Maybe in you have felt deep hurt, betrayal, anger, and on and on about an abuse you endured as a child. Those feelings spill out into your relationships every day until you get qualified help to deal with them. That baggage is too heavy and deep to unpack by yourself. It has to be unpacked, though, so you can leave behind the feelings that you had to stuff and let them be in the abuser's baggage where they belong. Of course you feel angry and bitter toward the person(s) who betrayed you! Those feelings are valid and unfortunately you had to have them, but you don't have to keep them.

Let's take Ephesians 4:31 apart—unpack it, if you will allow a little pun. Actually, forget the pun; it's time to be serious and deeply look at some hard stuff. Get a box of tissues—hopefully you'll look honestly and closely enough to need them. Keep in mind Ephesians 4:31 doesn't say we are never to feel these feelings; sometimes they are absolutely justified and even necessary, but we're to deal with them and "put away". Don't shove them back into the baggage, but put away. Away, as in gone, on a long trip with no return date. The first step to do that is to look at them with bold honesty.

This brings us to time for another exercise. On a large piece of paper, draw a piece of baggage. Make it look like an actual open suitcase of some sort. It can be a detailed drawing complete with lots of zippers and pockets or it can be a simple three-straight-line creation. In some manner which is meaningful to you, put in your suitcase all the unhealthy, crushing things you pack each and every day to take into the world. Pack all the clamor, anger and slander and bitterness. Don't focus on the actions but on the feelings you've held onto all these years about the actions. You can draw symbols that represent the contents, or write actual words, or even be creative and glue pictures, etc. into your suitcase. It's probably unproductive to list every painful incident in your life. Who could ever do that anyway? Just list/draw/glue the gist of the contents of your baggage. For example, it's unnecessary to list each and every time your alcoholic mother hurled hatred at you. Instead, note something like these examples:

- "I felt belittled and like trash when my mother would………"
- I 'M SO CONFUSED AND ENRAGED BECAUSE MY UNCLE HURT ME LIKE THAT AND NOBODY HELPED ME"
- "For too long I have felt useless because I believed the lie for years my boss told me so long ago about…….."

- Remember to include valid, self-earned beliefs in your baggage, like:
- "I'm so mad at myself for not standing up to the bully"
- "I feel like such a failure for losing my wife 5 years ago due to my affair or addiction."

Take your time with this exercise. It's of pivotal importance to your future relationships. This is where you face truth, not the slander someone else threw at you and you were forced to hold onto for too long.

MY BAGGAGE

Okay, when you think you are finished and your ugly bag is packed, go even deeper. Look at everything you wrote, drew or glued in your "bag" and go deeper into your feeling about it. Think about how you unpack these feelings from your "bag" every day and bring them with you into every interaction. We do it mindlessly, like we're pulling our ham sandwich out of our lunch bag. Just as we use the sandwich for body fuel, we can also use the anger as fuel to distance ourselves from others, or to fuel our self-protective barrier by distracting us. These distractions keep us from true fellowship with Him and other people. This is why God does not want anger, wrath, lies, clamor or malice to be part of us, His amazing creation!

So... bitterness. A definition I found on Google is "lack of sweetness" which is an excellent way to look at the word but it goes oh so much deeper, does it not? It often shoots right past a lack of sweetness and catapults into resentment, anger, and simmering rage. It can even turn inward and become depression, anxiety, suicidality, homicidality, you name it. It is straight out of hell, and our "roaring lion" enemy

LOVES how the bitterness he causes devours us from the inside out.

It is almost unavoidable that, probably as a very little, sweet child, you took a mean-spirited hurt thrown at you from a sibling, mean neighbor kid or—much harder—a parent and put it into a container in your heart. You really had no option but to "bag it" since you didn't have the skills or outlet to adequately deal with it. Maybe openly expressing the hurt would actually bring you another slap or angry word, so you made sure to close that bag as tightly as possible. The next jab, betrayal or wounding came at you and, still unable to deal constructively with it, you added it to the bag. You do this over your lifetime, and the bag becomes heavier than you can carry. You've been so busy stuffing the hurts into your bag that you too rarely stop to get rid of anything in the bag. Seriously—when is the last time you reached into your "bag" of hurts that made you store up bitterness, looked at an incident that you put in there, and dealt with your feelings about it once and for all? It's time to clear out the bag of bitterness. You certainly don't need it and it is crushing you.

Next in the bag in our Scriptural picture is wrath and anger. Well (forgive me here, Christians whose words may be purer than mine) hell, yes we are angry and wrathful! Someone hurt us and we have had no choice but to store it all up! Why wouldn't anyone be angry when, for horrible instance, the person who was supposed to love and protect them struck out at them for no other reason than because they could and it seemed to the abuser a good way to expel some of the their own bitterness?

Did you know that we rarely feel pure anger? Anger is almost always rooted in fear. Yep, next time you're angry or in a wrathful tantrum stop and get deeply honest about why you are so angry. I bet you a Krispy Kreme glazed donut it's because something about the situation terrifies you. It's likely you have a sense you're not in control of the tantrum-worthy situation and that is so very scary. Or a "trigger," an incident that reminded you of a long-ago trauma over which you had no control, occurred and some of that anger came bursting out of the bag as a cover for the vulnerability you feel.

Not long ago, I had a major melt-down tantrum which sure looked and sounded like anger, but it was really deep fear. I had a "date' to babysit a five year old so her parents could have a date night, so I carefully scheduled my time, left early, was cruising nicely along, until I wasn't . There was a jam that turned out to be two and a half hours long. So much for careful scheduling. I eventually exited the highway and called my long-suffering husband to help me navigate. There was shrill, hysterical screaming involved that sounded a lot like my voice. Before that conversation was over, I made a U-turn that crossed five lanes, veering so sharply my cell phone flew to regions unknown in my car and, boy, did my husband ever get an earful of what his sweet wife says when he's not around! Since I assumed surely the phone, hurled to nether regions of my car, was disconnected, I just let my words rip and it was u-g-l-y. Yes, I was mad at the universe for making me late, but what was really underneath my 'anger' was deep fear that my parents were right and in fact I wasn't enough, I was basically useless, there was no escaping that, and no matter what I did or how hard I tried I wouldn't meet the standard for acceptability. Terrified me to my core, so I had to put up the shield of rage to protect my vulnerable core. I do this often, unfortunately.

Since God doesn't want us to be fearful, we have to put it away. It is extremely helpful to look at your anger through the lens of fear. Once you figure out and admit that you're in fact very fearful of something rather than angry, the anger will have no place in you anymore. Once I stopped panting in my car and looked at the situation through the proper lens I was able to put away the anger and begin to deal with the fear. I'm still working on that, as well as the sheepishness I feel for the tantrum that I subjected my shocked husband to, but I'm on the right track now. In looking at the reality of the emotional situation, I can achieve a resolution. I can't put away anger if it is in fact something else.

Not all anger is directed outward. Some anger is directed inward, to our own selves. Please, please, please look at this honestly. How much truth does that statement hold for you? Have you worked through the anger you felt toward yourself when you fumbled the football in the play-off game in the 11th grade? Are you angry at yourself because you couldn't stop the abuse your step-dad inflicted on your mom, siblings or you? Are you berating yourself for screwing up the interview for the perfect job? God tells us to let that all go as well. This can be so hard, because often self-directed anger is in our very core and to lose it would feel like we were empty, without our life-long companion. Who will we be, what will protect us if we don't have the shield of anger to hold in front of us 24/7? Competent counselors can help you work through the anger you hold so close. Please find one! You're worth it, and the people around you want you to set aside your anger!

"Clamor." Wow, there's a word right out of Hell. It means a loud, constant confusing noise. Think jackhammers, a tornado, an arguing couple, shrieking fire alarms, screeching two year olds in a restaurant….all at the same time, at varying decibels. Think of a time when you were in such an environment. Not enjoyable, right? Remember, we were made to frolic in a glorious, lovingly-made Earth over which we had significant dominion, not for such a thing as clamor! Clamor robs us of our ability to rest, think, play, and enjoy. It is all-consuming and horrible, but it is part of our baggage because there is endless noise in our heads. Perhaps you 'hear' damaging words said to you in the past, your own confusion and hurt over what someone else did to you or that life threw at you, grief over a dreadful loss, uncertainty about future decisions, and so forth. It seems like it never stops. Yet we're called to stop it and to put it away. While a counselor would be an excellent way to work through your clamor, there can also be profound benefit asking for help from the capital-C Counselor, the Spirit who God gives us to connect us to Him. You can learn so much and therefore master your clamor by asking to be shown by the Spirit what your clamor is, from where it originates, and how to quiet it.

Next in our Ephesians-inspired bag is slander, the making of false statements which harm a reputation or paint someone in a negative manner. Bald-faced lies, basically. God does not want us to do this to others, obviously, but I also believe He hates it when we do it to ourselves. We lie to ourselves all the time when we absorb other people's lies about us. For instance, if a parent told you as a child that you were ugly, worthless, or unlovable, it would be easy for you to believe the lie, considering the source. If you don't ever shed that belief, you're slandering yourself and God tells us not to do that. God is truth all the time, always. No false belief is ever okay with Him and should never be a part of one of His much-loved children, but it so often and pervasively and insidiously is.

When you looked more deeply into your bags, what emotions were there? Look at those emotions with a microscope (and preferably a qualified counselor!) and see if they're emotions which truly "belong" to you. We've been taught for decades all our emotions are valid, precious things which many of us practically worship, but I'm going to veer somewhat and suggest that some of the long-baggaged emotions may actually be invalid. Yep, I propose that much of what you feel may not even be yours to feel!

If you feel shame for hiding your baby sister's Bunny-kins that night almost two decades ago and making her cry because she couldn't sleep, yeah… that's yours. You earned that shame and you have to deal with that until you reach a healthy resolution, then put it away. Feel shame for choosing to cheat on your spouse? That's yours, too. Bad choices should earn shame, no matter what the current "everything we do is okay" cultural trend. But, if you felt shame throughout middle school because you smelled bad because your family had no money for plumbing and no one took care of you because they were all high and drunk, that's not your shame. It's false shame for you. You never earned it. It happened to you and it was bad, but it isn't yours. Someone else earned the shame of causing you to be caught up in a life that resulted in odor clinging to you and the other kids being mean to you. You had to bear it, but you didn't create it. There is no truth in you holding onto that shame and it is slanderous to tell yourself otherwise. If, though, as a result of that horrid upbringing you choose to get on drugs and steal to support your habit, then yes, that is your shame. That which we do not choose is not our shame. Get away from the lie that says otherwise. That's Satan's voice you hear telling you that you are dirty, useless, etc. and you should be ashamed of yourself and the person you are. He's lying to you and slandering you—don't put this in your baggage! Our wonderful Father holds us accountable only for our actions, not what others do to us.

Similarly, if you were head cheerleader and led your squad to victory at Nationals, you can't put this in a bag and unpack it daily as smugness or superiority. That's arrogance, and it doesn't go well in a healthy relationship and needs to be put away. It is slander. Leading a team to a win doesn't make you better than anyone. And, frankly, no one cares (actually that could just be my high school geek girl slipping out, sorry). It's slander to think more highly of ourselves than we ought. It's okay and healthy to acknowledge you were a great cheerleader but to adopt an air of superiority over others is a lie-you're not. That promotion or raise you got or the big award your child got is great and congratulations and back-slaps are in order, but don't pack that in a bag marked "Reasons Why I'm Awesomer Than Anyone Else And Therefore Entitled" because that's slanderous thinking. Put it away.

Lastly, we have malice. It makes me feel kind of sad to have to deal with this one because although I never ever engage in malicious actions (it's true, I really don't) I LOVE my private, malicious thoughts.

Oh, how they comfort me, build me up and entertain me. If a celebrity or politician I don't care for gets his or her comeuppance of some kind, how gleeful I am when I talk about it, clicking my tongue and shaking my head! If I ever get wind of the bad fortune—even death!—of the person who wronged a family member many years ago I'll maliciously rejoice! I can spend hours thinking maliciously about the HOA, my exes, nasty neighbors I used to have, a boss who was unfair, and on and on. At one point I even had a list of people I felt malice toward! That shames me to my core now but for a fleeting moment it made sense somehow. I probably even enjoyed adding names to the list, but it is so hideously ugly that I was pretty quick to give it to Jesus because it was such a heavy burden on my heart to have to carry around. No wonder God tells us to get rid of it! Yuck!

Malice is defined as a desire to do evil or harm. Yeah, I have that desire occasionally, and I work on putting it away as God commands. I need to work harder; heart-sin issues are so much harder to dispel than action-sin issues! Maybe you are a kind wonderful person who never has such thoughts. I envy you. I may even be tempted to be mad at you for not providing a reason for me to think maliciously of you! (I so hope you're nodding your heads, knowing exactly what I am talking about!) Most of us probably have some malice in us, no matter what we call it or how we pretty it up. Road rage? It's malice. Crazy parents at kids' games who yell at refs? Yep, that's deep-rooted malice.

Where does malice come from? I don't know. I think it varies for everyone. Is it a reaction to childhood abuse, or learned from our critical, malicious parents or 'simply' a selfish attitude of extreme arrogance that makes us feel entitled to harbor such horrid thoughts? The malice I hold is pure selfishness. Thinking mean thoughts about people makes me feel justified, correct in my choices, and puts a barrier of sorts between me and my critics' darts. It also keeps a wall between me and others, which is exactly the opposite of what I want. Pointless, isn't it? Ridiculous, even, but there it is.

There's one more aspect of Ephesians 4:31—the "put away" part. We 've looked deeply into ourselves to find and identify the bitterness, wrath, anger, clamor, slander, and malice, which wasn't easy or pleasant. Now we see it more clearly. But what do we DO with it? HOW do we put it away? Identifying baggage and calling it what it is and understanding its source is helpful, but now what?

Even God cannot remove what happened to make us feel such horrible things right out of Hell itself. The past happened, and no amount of praying can change it. What we can and must change is our reaction to our baggage. God is all over this one. He saw it coming! Our Creator didn't leave us defenseless in this world against these things. He has given us His Spirit, who is the complete opposite of bitterness, wrath, anger, clamor, slander, and malice. God expects us to ask His Spirit to help us put away what we must because He understands we can't do it on our own. We had help putting those things into our hearts, so how could we get rid of them by ourselves?

You can't possibly put away the Ephesians 4:31 bad guys unless you ask first for wisdom. Wisdom is essential to see these things clearly and discern they are what they are. If you don't see the evil in your baggage how can you possibly ask for each piece to be removed? How do you ask this? It's pretty easy, actually, and the outcome is guaranteed. God is quick to give wisdom when we ask. James 1:5 tells those who lack wisdom (everyone at one time or another!) to faithfully ask God who will generously and without reproach give it. Boom! Done! THAT is the Father we love. He is generously and, presumably, delightedly giving us the good things we faithfully ask for, so we can look more like Jesus.

I adore the words used here—generously and without reproach. I love generosity. I remember my grandmother generously gave me cookies just because....well, because they were cookies, and I was her beloved granddaughter! In hindsight, I must admit, she may have been more generous about giving me the cookies that I made that would look goofy on her pretty tray at Christmas. But, she also let me have the beautiful wreath or bell cookies she made, not just the three-legged green reindeer or naked Santa ones I'd made. Yes, I know naked Santa cookies are just weird but I thought they were hilarious. I was eight. The point is that being on the receiving end of generosity is wonderful. It's may be the best expression of love ever! AND, we get what we're asking for—wisdom-- without reproach! So, we get the cookies without being told we shouldn't be so greedy, or our teeth will rot, or our dinner will be spoiled! When we ask God for wisdom He doesn't chide us for not knowing stuff already and having to ask, as parents undoubtedly and perhaps unthinkingly might've. Nope, He just hands it out. Generously!

So, when you faithfully ask God for wisdom to enable you to put away the bitterness, wrath, anger, clamor, slander and malice, does it just come to your heart and you're washed clean and done with it? Maybe, but it seems like that's a faulty expectation. I don't know of many people who were simply delivered from their darkest attitudes in an instant, but I know hundreds of people who are working, with the Spirit, toward that goal of being free. You can be sure, because you're promised in James 1:5, that you'll receive wisdom from God if you ask Him in faith, but He might expect you to do some work to get the most wisdom He offers.

The first gift of wisdom He gives might be the wisdom to know where to go looking and to have the courage to follow through on that search. There are countless books, seminars and counselors who are Christ-centered, godly sources of wisdom. Wander through a library or Christian bookstore in the Psychology section and you may be amazed at the resources God puts in your path.

Another gift is the wisdom to keep unpacking your baggage, even when it hurts so badly. There's so much to unpack---childhood hurts and abuses, hurts and betrayals in adulthood, lies you were told and forced to believe, addictions-- either your own or someone's close to you--, generational family secrets, disappointments, failures—again, either your own or someone else's—and on and on and on. The list may seem like you're endlessly pulling ugly things out of the bag and that you'll never be out of the counselor's office for good, but hold strong! Keep unpacking! The cost is too high to keep all the reasons for your bitterness, wrath, anger, clamor, slander and malice stuffed in your baggage.

What is the cost for not unpacking the pains you've stuffed into your suitcases? We see it all the time, every day, all around us. It includes:

- Feeling like you deserve bad things and settling for them
- An unhealthy lifestyle which can be anything from drug addiction, smoking, alcoholism, over or under eating, sex addictions or integrity issues, and so much more.
- Anger outbursts toward others. Maybe even violence
- Running away from the pain using more "acceptable" compulsions/addictions like shopping, gambling, care-taking others, hoarding things to create a barrier, and on and on.
- Depression
- Lying. Especially to yourself
- A critical spirit toward others. Haughtiness
- Allowing others to cheat, betray, you and generally poo on you time and time again
- My personal un-favorite—chasing after relationship after relationship hoping to un-do what you have packed. It won't, but it'll cost you dearly and you won't see it until it's too late.

- Name your own here. Seriously, take a moment to honestly answer this for yourself.

Clearly, we are meant to get rid of anything that holds us back from frolicking with God like we were created to do. We must put it away. Now.

CHAPTER 5-- BE A PERSON WHO CAN HANDLE THEIR MONEY

"Whaaat?" you ask? THIS belongs in a book about relationships? Yup, because if you can't handle your relationship with a dollar bill you cannot handle a relationship with a person.

You've probably heard that money and possessions are mentioned a lot in the Bible—over 800-2300 times depending on who's counting and if they include verses about topics like contentment and greed and debt, etc. It must be pretty important.

Healthy, mature handling of our money requires many of the same attitudes and practices as maintaining a strong relationship. Whether you have a lot of money or a little, it is yours and you must make sure it meets your needs including keeping bills paid, tithing, and, hopefully, helping others in need when necessary.

Think about it. What makes someone a good manager of their money? They are a steady worker, not greedy, able to be patient about what they want rather than needing every whim immediately gratified.

They are also wise, responsible about paying off loans, not frivolous or careless, and so forth. Aren't these exactly the characteristics an adult should bring to the relationship table?

I gave birth to two daughters and fostered several others. My birth daughters couldn't be more different regarding money. Although both me and their father are quite frugal and not prone to over-spending, one daughter cannot save her money to save her soul. (Good thing it doesn't!) She is an excellent worker, has been solidly employed since she was 16 and she makes sure her bills are paid automatically which is great! That shows a lot of character and maturity. But, she has no real brain-knowledge about money. She rarely knows how much is in her bank account, and she literally keeps about ten pounds of loose change in her purse, and shops without boundaries. She will have to dramatically change her habits in order to buy the condo she says she wants. That means, no $200 haircuts and $40 + tip (which may be $20, depending on how she feels that day, because she doesn't actually calculate what the correct tip should be) manicures or lunches out. She has many wonderful qualities, but so far, good money management is not one of them. My other daughter squeezes a penny so tightly I swear you can hear Abe whimper, as opposed to the gleeful giggling to be heard as he twirls merrily out of my spender-daughter's wallet. The penny-pincher, like her sister, has been an excellent worker and has gotten a solid career off to a good start, but her approach to money is very different. She searches for hours on second-hand selling sites for all her furniture and some of her clothing and footwear, she shops almost exclusively at thrift stores, makes homemade Christmas gifts, and so on. She is cheap, but she pulls it off like a champ. She knows her bank account balance and her student loan accounts to the dollar. She's almost fearful of spending. Her own money, that is; she seemed quite happy spending mine!

So, what kind of relationship histories would you guess for these young women? You'd be correct if you guessed the spender never quite has her feet in a solid relationship, but rather she lands in them, blinking and looking around. She over-gives and under-gets. This, predictably, leads to her feeling frustrated and used.

She is also without the things she "bought" with her time, efforts, and affections, like a caring boyfriend who's there for her, treats her with respect and love for the delight she is. The daughter who saves has had, in measured succession, nice boyfriends who are each a little more mature and awesome than the last. She's gaining experience so she will recognize 'the one.' She's saving up the knowledge and experience she gains with each dating experience.

Having good brain-knowledge of money is a necessity. It's essential to your stability and speaks of your maturity level when you have a savings account, bills paid, and the end of your credit card debt within sight.

Take a moment to honestly think about how you manage your money.

- What's in your wallet? Do you have too many credit cards? Are too many of them close to the max?
- Do you feel confident in this area, with a growing savings account?
- When's the last time you tithed as we're told to do, or gave to a charity?

- Would your family and friends say you live within your means? Do you fully understand what "your means" are? Do you feel like you live within them?
- Would anyone accuse you of being cheap, overly tight or frugal?
- Do you live a life of chasing money? Do you place too much value on money at the expense of things like relationships, humility, or building a good character instead of a large bank balance? Are you greedy?
- Do you find that you are often in need, borrowing from people, or sleeping on friends' couches because you didn't pay your rent again?
- Do you frequently over-buy gifts, dinners out, etc. for your friends and family?
- Are you an emotional spender? Do you frequently do "retail therapy", try to buy affection from others, or "help" people by bailing them out again and again?
- Are you easy to take advantage of? Are you likely to fall for a scam involving a "prince" in

Nigeria who needs you to send him $5,000 so he can get out of jail? Or the co-worker who promises to pay you back but never does?

- If your income is low or limited, are you doing everything you can to increase it, by looking into part-time jobs, getting more education, or providing a good or service from home?

If after pondering these and other money-related questions, compare your answers to your ability to BE the person you want to be who's healthy and ready for a meaningful relationship. Are there any gaps? Do you see a connection? If not, ask your trusted family and friends if they think there's a connection between your money management and relationship history. You can talk to a bank employee who'll take the time to talk with you about managing your expenditures, savings, etc.

A relative who happens to be horrible with her money taught me a fitting and valuable phrase: respect your money. She meant to take the time to put my credit card or change safely back into my wallet immediately without carelessly dropping it in and hoping I can find it later. This is excellent advice, but appropriate respect of money goes even further.

You owe yourself the dignity and care of respecting the financial gifts God has given you. He didn't have to equip you for employment or however you get income, but He did. It is 800-2300 times important, and everyone brings their management of and beliefs about money into any relationship.

CHAPTER 6-- BE A PERSON WHO TAKES CARE OF THEIR HEALTH

This one seems obvious, right? If we don't respect ourselves enough to do the best we can in all areas of our health, how can we expect anyone else to respect and care for us? True, not everyone has access to tip-top insurance for all their physical, dental, vision, and mental health needs, but the key phrase is "do your best."

Physical

Assuming you have adequate insurance, do you take the time to meet your needs? We're all so busy and it's almost impossible to find the time and energy for a yearly physical, and it's a giddy relief when we put off a mammogram or other dreaded exam, or even postpone a teeth cleaning. But it is so important to keep up with maintenance of our bodies. You know it is.

It's like the flight attendants say prior to take-off about the masks dropping down from the compartment overhead: you must put on your own mask before you are ready to help anyone else. Pre-kids, I always thought of course I wouldn't do it that way, that surely I'd put the masks over their scared little faces before even thinking of myself, but that's actually quite stupid. It wouldn't help my babies one bit if I passed out from wrestling with them to put on a mask. Nope, that just means we'd all be goners. If I prioritize myself in that situation, we're all going to be okay. The kids will see me wearing it and they will follow suit much more easily and let me put it on them. Likewise, if I have taken care of all my physical needs to the best of my ability, others will be more likely to follow suit and take care of me, not betraying, disrespecting or abusing me.

So take a second and think about what, if any, gaps you have right now in your personal care. Is it time for a physical, a trip to the dentist, or time to get your eyes checked? Is it—gulp and head-down-for-a-second—time for one of those less pleasant exams? Men, is it time to cough on cue? Women, is it time to face the horrifying stirrups? Did your doctor recommend you follow up with something and you haven't gotten around to it? Be honest with yourself about what's kept you from taking care of these issues, and resolve it now! Waiting for "something" won't help your physical health one bit and it puts you further away from your goal! Take a baby step if you must, like making (and keeping!) a commitment to get one important health issue taken care of each month, or even each quarter. Make and stick to a commitment to care for the body you were given.

We talked about weight from an appearance perspective in Chapter 3, but how about health-wise? Have you attained and maintained a good, healthy weight? Congratulations if you have! I'm envious, but I congratulate you on your efforts. If you can't say that you've attained and maintained well, why not? Seriously, why aren't you at the weight range your doctor or the weight charts say you should be? Look at this earnestly and honestly. If weight is a problem for you consider if your weight is controlled by:

- Medication?
- Over or under exercising?
- Over or under eating?
- Poor food choices?
- Heredity?
- Age that you haven't adjusted for?

- Not cooking at home and relying too much on take-out?
- An eating disorder that you haven't gotten help for? (DO IT NOW)
- Just plain lack of motivation or—shall I say it?-- even laziness? Why?
- Emotions?

Emotions can be a huge factor in our weight. If a person is depressed, for instance, they don't feel like getting up and dressed, getting in the car, going to the gym, and then using those galling machines. We all pretty much know that, but what about other emotional stops to a good weight? What about anxiety, fear or the need for comfort? What, if any, emotions get in the way of living at the weight that's healthy and comfortable for you?

Did you know that it's fairly common for a person to gain large amounts of weight as a result of sexual abuse? Very sad but true. Victims of rape or molestation often develop the habit of eating for comfort; a big bowl of chips or ice cream several times a day can provide a whole lot of momentary pleasure when pleasure or comfort is hard to come by otherwise. Unhealthy eating can seem to be a bandage for the body that was violated so cruelly. Excess weight can also seem like a barrier; "If I weigh 700 pounds no one can push me around easily." It can even seem like a good plan to make the survivor feel "ugly" or undesirable to a predator. Of course, sexual abuse or exploitation is about control, evil and hurt people hurting other people, rage, and aggression and has nothing to do with physical attractiveness, but survivors often grasp at this straw. Having a sense of control is far better than being completely vulnerable, even if the sense of control is errant. This misuse of food is an understandable reaction, but it's also self-defeating and deceiving. It hands the last word on our health and safety over to the abuser, which is exactly what the victim tries to avoid in the first place! If you struggle in this area, please get help. Don't give your abuser more of you than what he/she has already ripped away. You had no choice at the time of the abuse, but you do now. You really do.

You have the power to get yourself to a healthier weight. No one else has it. Use it well. There is no downside to making your scale your cheering, supportive friend.

Disability

Do you have a noticeable disability or challenge that makes you feel "less than" or undesirable? I'm so sorry you're living this way! Maybe you use a walker, are in a wheelchair, have a prosthesis or a scar or any of a hundred situations that might have made you a target for teasing or a poor self image.

You know what? Live it proudly! As much as it's possible, lift your head, straighten your posture, and make good eye contact! Smile and ask people about themselves, show interest in people around you. Laugh. Your disability is part of who you are and you have every right and responsibility to present yourself in the best manner possible. You matter, of course, and can be every bit as ready to BE the right person as anyone else. Don't ever think otherwise, no matter what. Everything in this book—and in life!—applies to you equally, no matter what you've been led to believe. You developed innovative ways to deal with obstacles, and I hope you are proud and confident of your ability to do so. Confidence is what people will notice even before they see a wheelchair or cane!

Mental/Emotional

We will never be free of every bit of emotional pain, embarrassment or fear. However, we cannot expect to BE the right person for a healthy relationship until and unless we have controlled those emotions and stop letting them control us!

We've all—'fess up here—watched a tasteless talk show episode full of salacious details about a woman who stayed with her man even after he shot her in the eye, or a man who stays with his girlfriend after she sleeps with his brother AND his best friend AND their deacon, etc. Watching shows like that makes us feel better about ourselves, until they don't. Until we realize, while not so outrageous as these stories, our story might be similar at its core. Too often we feel stuck or pulled into patterns that are harmful, unhealthy and destructive. Why do we do that? Why do we feel that that's all we deserve?

There are so many reasons why many of us aim for the low-hanging fruit on the Tree of Mate Material. Perhaps we believed the lies that we aren't desirable, we're dirty, we deserve to be alone, we're not good enough, we're ugly, etc. etc. etc. Those lies come from our enemy through people who did not or could not have our best interests at heart. They're probably even more wounded than us, so why listen to them?

But we do listen to the filth. We take those horrific ideas into our heart and hold them there, despite all the words to the contrary found in God's letter to us which tells us how very worthwhile and loveable we are to Him. He loves us to the point of trading His life for ours as a bridge so He doesn't have to spend eternity without us. THAT is the only thought we need to hold. But too often we nurture the lies, because to hold onto them gives us a barrier against risking hurt like the rejection we expect or—God forbid—confirmation that all the lies are true and we are proven to in fact be worthless. It seems easier to keep the barrier rather than take the risk.

This heart-deep barrier can almost never be removed on our own. We need help, and lots of it, to get past this damage and to hear God's thoughts of us and the amazing truth that we are God-breathed.

Have you done everything you can do to get beyond the hurts and imbalances that hold you back? Have you read the books, studied the Scripture and sought the good counseling available? Are you on the right anti-anxiety, anti-depression or anti-whatever meds you need?

Please put this book down right now if you're someone who says "I don't need medication because God will heal me of the gut-clamping anxiety I feel every day and it's wrong to take medicine when I should be faithful and wait for healing. I'll just suffer until He delivers me." Put the book down because I need a break from you, and you need a break from me while I deal with my frustration. Deep breath. Another. Okay, ready.

The idea that we as Christians should not use the meds God has gifted us with to deal with mental and emotional health issues is a lie right out of Hell. Nothing makes our enemy laugh harder than when we're held back from being who we were created to be and doing for His Kingdom what we were created to do because we're listening to one of his lies! I hate making the enemy laugh and I refuse to voluntarily have weak spots and gaps for his guffaws. Don't make Satan laugh at your mental health issues. Prayerfully get help with it so the issue is managed and you can move onward and upward! God's deliverance from these issues may in fact be in pill form or in the form of a qualified counselor. Take the help He has designed for you. Steve Arterburn, pastor, author, and host of radio Christian counseling talk show 'New Life Live', is wise to say, "Don't wait for God to do what He is waiting for you to do!"

Social

Humans are designed to be in community with other humans. We probably all know Scriptural references that tell us this..."It is not good for man to be alone" (Genesis 2:18) and "...if one falls down his companion can lift him up but woe to him who is alone when he falls and has not another to lift him up" (Ecclesiastes 4:10) and the one about a cord of three strands not being easily broken (Ecclesiastes 4:12), and so on.

Why? Why did God mandate we strand together? Why does someone else have to lift me up when it was my own dumb fault I tripped over the sidewalk because I was looking at the squirrel? Can't we just live independently and not be close to annoying, messy people? That seems so tempting at times doesn't it? Oh, maybe that's just me.

Well, I don't know why. I looked for an explanation in Genesis about why He made so many of us instead of creating us one at a time, or even stopping at Adam. The first mention I found of Him creating us is Genesis 1:26 where He uses the word "them" so I think we can believe it was His idea in the first place to make multiples of us and in fact to have the first "them" make even more of us (Genesis 1:28).

So, since we're now a "them" instead of our own individual universe, we must deal with other people and that's not easy all the time. In fact, life itself isn't easy all the time, which brings us to God's gracious gift of the need to be social. If we are alone we do not learn how to love or to receive love, which makes it much harder to love the One who made us which is what it's all about in the first place.

So, what's the best way to follow this mandate in this broken world full of broken people? Maybe the best bet is to find people with the same breaks as you.

Or maybe better yet, different breaks so you can help each other; you might have no trouble navigating around a pit that would cause me horrible harm, and vice versa.

To be socially healthy we must be connected to somebody or a group of somebodies. We need to see someone's face light up when we enter the room, or feel the warmth of a handshake or hug to know we're alive and that we matter! When is the last time you felt valued just because you were there? How long has it been since you felt your face move into a genuine smile instead of a forced one when you see someone? Make a list of those people by whom you feel valued, who know when you're in a 'pit' and know how to help you out of it.

PEOPLE WHO I FEEL VALUED BY

Did you discover any surprises as you made your list? Fewer than you thought? More than you expected?

Just for fun once I tried to make a list of 100 people I actually know (as opposed to celebrities or historical figures, etc.) that I would truly and wholly enjoy spending an evening with, with absolutely no qualms or negatives. I thought it would be a quick activity but I was wrong-o! I didn't make it past 43 people! Being a decade or so older now hopefully my list would at least make it into the 80's but this activity still makes me wonder about my own connectedness. I feel connected—I'm married and have adult children, I have three or four very best friends and several friendships still blooming and a couple dozen co-workers who answer me when I ask about their weekend, but still I didn't make it past 43! Am I really connected in the way God wants me to be? Maybe my presence in a room isn't enough, and I have to go deeper.

On the night before He died Jesus wanted His friends to support Him in his deep grief and distress. He took them with Him, told them how grieved He was and just asked them to stay with Him and "keep watch with Him" (Matthew 26:36). Well, they didn't last an hour. They stayed with Him, but they didn't keep watch as He'd asked because they fell asleep. Three times. As I see this scene in my mind, I think Peter, James, and John meant to be connected to Jesus and maybe they believed they were being good solid friends. After all, they were present "in the room." They didn't get it. They weren't able to go deep enough and truly connect to His angst. They simply didn't know how to help Him. I imagine the first time Jesus woke them up they were embarrassed, but I wonder how they felt the second and third time He found them sleeping. I feel so bad for Jesus wanting so much to have comfort from His friends and they couldn't do it. He must've felt so alone and discouraged by these men who held such a special place in His heart.

If these three chosen men couldn't support the best friend they could ever imagine, who could? Humans no longer can connect like that; at Creation we could have perfect connectedness with each other and God, but then it crumbled. This scene makes me think Jesus may have hoped somehow the closeness at Creation could be rekindled (I know He knew it couldn't be) when He needed it most, but sin had gotten in the way.

So, here we are, limited in our capacity to be perfect in our ability to being close to others and to fully enjoy loving and being loved as it was intended, but we still must live in society with as much closeness and support as possible. Good news----God has written an entire book for us telling us how to do that through Jesus! We won't be—we can't be—perfect at it until we're in Heaven where there is no sin, no discord, and no breaks, but we can still connect to others in a meaningful way through the Holy Spirit and the instructions given to us in the Bible, from counselors or life coaches.

Spiritual

Spiritual health. This could be a short segment because, even after more than 45 years of walking through life with Jesus, I have no idea what this term even means. His love, who He is, and how He thinks is too huge for my brain to grasp, as it should be! What good is a God I could understand fully? HOW does a person say they've acquired spiritual health with the perfect Creator of the universe and the One whose love for us went to and past the very end of Himself on earth?

Maybe spiritual health simply means that you have latched on to three simple truths:

- There is a God, a Supreme Being who created the universe and everything in it, down to the nth detail.
- I am not it. I'm not God, Master of all. I can do nothing on my own. Nothing. I cannot think without the brain He designed for me. I cannot speak without the vocal cords He gave me. I cannot make a single bean grow in my garden without the seed, soil, rain, and sun that He put in place. I didn't hang the sun and moon exactly where they needed to be hung to sustain life on Earth, and I certainly cannot replicate human life on my own. Any thought I have of self-reliance is nonsense.
- Since there is a God, I'd better figure out Who He is and what He wants, then live my

> life accordingly. Nothing other than the Biblical explanation of God makes sense. I've found no other religion that explains creation adequately because only the Judeo/Christian explanation also includes the Creator wanting human beings and going out of His way to wonderfully and thoughtfully form us. In an adequate explanation about the Creation of the universe and everything in it, there must also be love or nothing about the explanation makes sense. Since both the Old Testament and the New Testament speak sentence by sentence of a love far beyond anything I can imagine or produce, I'm going with the God of the Bible.

In a moment I will suggest you take a minute and write down the premises on which you base your life spiritually. Of course I'm not saying we all have our own "truths" and we can fabricate truth at will. Truth is truth. But, your wording might be quite different from mine. Spending some time figuring out and expressing succinctly what your beliefs are must be the first step in finding any type of health in spirituality.

Maybe the way you've expressed a spiritual basis is different than how I've expressed it, but the result has to be the same. To be spiritually healthy we must know concisely and definitely what our faith is, and we must live that faith every second, albeit imperfectly. Our faith MUST be in something or, preferably, Someone, far larger than ourselves, and completely outside of our capacity to fully understand. Otherwise, our faith is really in ourselves and it is as worthless as the dust on my TV stand. Faith has to tell us how to live our lives bountifully, who we are and who we need to be, what relationships to have and how to have them meaningfully, and how to be equipped for death since life as we know it on this earth is finite. This is huge and requires a huge God.

Once you land on the truth of your existence, what you do with it produces health or frailty. If your faith is a frail faith you're "like a wave of the sea, blown and tossed by the wind," (James 1:6) or poorly rooted as in the parable Jesus told of the sower (Luke

8:13). To be strong and healthy in the Christian faith, follow the teachings of the Bible, including:

- Answer your door when Jesus knocks (Revelation 3:20), invite Him in, and begin the "dining" adventure you were meant to have for now and forever
- Meet with other believers regularly
- Pray without ceasing
- Repent of sins and "sin no more"
- "Be still and know that I am God." (Psalm 46:10)

Hmmm, most of the things the Bible tells us to do for a good relationship with Him can also be useful in having healthy relationships with people. Except for being still and awed in God's presence with knowledge of Who He is, the paragraph above not only describes the steps to having a great relationship with God, it also lays out the blueprints for having a strong relationship with another person. Spend time with others ("meet regularly with"), have meaningful and respectful conversation and always-open communication lines ("pray without ceasing") don't do hurtful and harmful things to the other person ("sin no more"). Funny how He worked that out for us.

When a lawyer (it's ok to insert a lawyer joke here just for fun) asks Jesus in Matthew 22:36 which is the great commandment of the Law, there's no indication that Jesus had to pause and think about His answer. He answered, presumably immediately, the most important thing in life is to "Love the Lord, Your God with all your heart, and with all your soul, and with all your mind." (Matthew 22:37) He makes sure to follow that up--again, presumably immediately-- with the second most important one which is, "You shall love your neighbor as yourself" (Matthew 22:39). These two commandments, prioritized and emphasized as they are, are the pillars upon which all spiritual and relational health depend.

Can we ever be 100 percent spiritually healthy? Can we ever say we've acquired complete health in this area? Nope, I don't think so because to say that I'm spiritually healthy means I perfectly, completely and always-every-second-of-every-day love God with all my being, and genuinely love others. Well, I think by now it's clear that I don't love like that on my best day. There is frailty in even my strongest moments of love toward God and certainly toward others. But, I can say that I'm moving toward a healthy, full relationship with God, with His help. That's as close as any of us can get to spiritual health on this side of Heaven.

So, what are the spiritual premises on which you base your life? You surely have a few. Whether you believe the highest power on earth is the God of the Bible, money, yourself, Buddha, or the ceramic frog in your backyard, you have them. Take a moment to list them now.

SPIRITUAL LIFE PREMISES

CHAPTER 7-- BE A PERSON IN THE RIGHT CAREER

When you tell people about your job, is your head up or down? Are you happy with your career path? Have you made the effort to deeply think about what you want to do in life, what you want to contribute to the world, and pursued that goal? Or have you simply accepted whatever dead-end job came along because bills must be paid? If you're on the track that you want to be on, great!! You've worked hard to get there, no doubt, and should be proud and confident about it, so give yourself credit! I've met people who were quite thrilled to be a janitor and did that job proudly and well and spoke of their job in a confident, positive manner. I've also met quite a few people with what most would consider high-end jobs and their heads were down when they discussed what they did for a living because they were not happy with their contribution. You can probably think of someone who drifted into their family business or who went on the career path their parents wanted, or one they themselves thought would make them successful, but were never happy. It's difficult to BE a healthy person ready for a strong relationship if you aren't doing what makes you feel strong and confident.

We spend roughly one half of our waking hours working, so we'd best be reasonably happy about it. If you're not in a job that makes your head lift, your eyes sparkle and voice perk up when you speak about it, why not? Is there a valid reason you're not in that job, or getting the necessary education or training to do that job? Or have you believed a lie you weren't worthy of good goals or you'd probably fail at whatever you tried to do or be? Don't believe that lie! You know where it comes from! Take at least one step toward your dream job—your best YOU—and see where that step takes you. Ponder and explore the barriers you deeply and honestly believe limit you from having a career that fulfills you and makes you feel and confident. Examine the barriers for validity. Many of them probably aren't valid. Make an effort in the right direction could shatter those barriers. Make some calls to universities or job seeking organizations, or take some career-finding tests online. Do anything that enables you to lift your head and say "I am studying to be a_______________." Be on a path so, when people ask what you do, you lift your head and put confidence in your posture when you explain your chosen occupation. You can do this!

CHAPTER 8-- BE A PERSON WITH GOOD BOUNDARIES

This might raise your eyebrows a bit. You might be saying, "Hey, I'm not a yard or a county! Why do I need a strong boundary?" Because, to explain it in a rather artsy way, think of yourself as a beautiful yard to be protected and tended. Your "yard" shouldn't be trampled upon, or full of ruts or overgrown into the neighbor's yard. (Especially if you have an HOA—ugh! Big fine for overgrowth!) You want the healthiest, greenest, most appealing, and productive yard you can have. This requires a boundary in the form of a fence, does it not?

I used a search engine thingie to look up the definition of "boundary" and got some very interesting results. One of them said it's a "limit of activity" in the vicinity of a subject. That's an excellent definition for the purpose of this chapter. "Limiting the activities" of what happens to you should be taught in high school, if not middle school. Another excellent definition is "a line marking where one area ends and another begins." I could write an entire chapter on these two concepts alone!

So, let's look at "one area ending and another beginning." It is important in life and particularly in relationships to know where you end and another person begins. If you take on too much of someone else, you can lose yourself and your 'yard' is trampled. Nothing beautiful can be produced there. If you allow another person to take too much of you, then you also will likely lose your 'self' and you risk losing your yard altogether.

We often think of it as kindness or helpfulness to habitually step in and assume another person's problems or to rescue a person from some negative consequences, but it really isn't. We can help people to find their own way and be supportive as they fix their own problems but unhealthiness comes in when we assume these problems as our own. Similarly, it isn't romantic to depend completely on the shining-armor knight to save us from all peril. No, it's weak and we aren't created to be weak. We are created as individuals with our own feelings, thoughts and actions. When we trample another individual's 'yard', or allow an individual to trample our own, we disregard and disrespect where we begin and end, and the other individual's beginning and end.

Right now there's probably a scenario happening where an alcoholic husband is happily sleeping off his drunken stupor while his wife is up all night, pacing and wondering how she can fix the situation. She's wondering what she will say to his boss this time so he keeps his job, how she will explain to the kids that daddy isn't feeling well and needs to be left alone and what she will say to her mother-in-law when hubby doesn't join in for Sunday dinner at MIL's house. Do you see the problem? Wifey has assumed responsibility for hubby's actions. She's forgotten where he ends and she begins, and where she ends and he begins. This may sound like the great plan of "two becoming one" in a marriage, but it isn't. It is one person sucking the other into dysfunction. She's taken on the role of fixer, appeaser, excuser, etc. thinking it will calm the issue. She's forgone the roles she is meant to have in order to take on the roles of his dysfunction. This will NEVER produce good results. The problem is primarily his and no one else can fix his problem. She can only work on her own issues stemming from hubby's drinking. She needs to "begin" by putting a fence in the yard which says his irresponsible drinking will no longer be tolerated. Wifey can no longer allow her 'yard' to be trampled and violated. She needs to re-establish where she ends and hubby begins.

What about the "limit of activity" definition? Think about the activity of the people around you and what they do around, for and to you. Do people generally treat you respectfully, honoring and appreciating your actions, opinions, and feelings in a healthy way? I'm not suggesting every family member, co-worker, etc. should bow to your every demand, but do people at least listen to your requests? Do they tend to treat you as a dumping ground for everything from dirty laundry to total financial support to care-taking with no appreciation for your effort? Are you the one known for doing anything asked of them no matter what your schedule or plan? It is critical to the well-being of your 'yard'—that is, your very self---to limit activity to only that which is uplifting and productive.

If you're teary or squirming right now, this probably hit a nerve for you. Maybe you see in your own life people seem to take advantage of you regularly, and/or you do way too much for others for the wrong reasons. You might wonder how this happened. Who taught these people that you're not a real person, responsible for your actions only, and you will never say "no" to a request?

You did. Sadly, it's true. You sent out the memo. You taught people, without even realizing, that you exist largely for the rescue, pleasure, comfort, and ease. of everyone else, never yourself. You've assumed doormat status and it's been ok with you for however long it has been the case. Obviously, it's not healthy or good. It's certainly not conducive to the type of relationship you want.

The problem with having poor boundaries isn't that you live a life of sacrifice and helping others. The problem is you have the wrong idea about it. You haven't freely chosen to lay your life down and you didn't make the conscious decision to be okay serving others in one-sided relationships. There is no joy in your service. It's a burden and a failed connection strategy. Perhaps you feel you're not worth your own identity or it would be a critically lacking identity, or that it's safer to live under the guise of melting into other people rather than being your own person who requires respect.

Service to others is fabulous! It's what God says to do, and the entire example Jesus set. A look in the Gospels (Matthew, Mark Luke and John) reveals Someone who lived entirely to serve, both His Father and human beings. We read about almost endless scenes of Jesus teaching and healing people. Does this mean He had poor boundaries? Of course not. He is perfect, and His example is perfect! He knew who He was while He was on Earth dealing with people. He didn't have to assume our identities. He left His perfect "yard" and chose to be obedient to the plan His Father laid out, by entering the "yard" known as Earth where funny, smelly, silly, earnest, hungry, hopeful people lived. The plan was His yard, and He remained in it without fault.

So how do you build appropriate fencing so you have healthy boundaries? Should it be a charming, white picket, a concrete wall, a line in the dirt, wrought iron? What? And how? This is actually a pretty simple fix. It's simple, but not necessarily easy. It takes a lot of practice to speak up for yourself and learn to say "no"to those endless requests you've always said "yes" to before. It may take some counseling or at least reading up on the subject. (I heartily recommend reading the book "Boundaries: When to Say Yes; How to Say No to Take Control of Your Life" by Dr. Henry Cloud and Dr. John Townsend or a similar book that'll help get you started in setting up appropriate boundaries) It is relatively simple to dig up the root of this habit of having poor boundaries and plant a whole new flower bed, protected by the security of the proper boundary.

A nutshell version of how to have healthy boundaries so you can have healthy relationships is to gain clarity about what's yours to do and to then learn how to say "no" to requests that do not fall into that category. If you've faithfully read the chapters leading up to this one, you probably have a pretty strong sense of what your strengths are, and you can probably go forward with a much better idea of where you begin and where you end, but it will take practice and careful thought to see situations where it's necessary to respond with "No, I can't help with that this time."

Learning to build and maintain healthy boundaries is actually a thrillingly fun process because every time you appropriately say "no" you've freed yourself! You have put one more picket on your fence. You're building on your success each and every time you refuse to be absorbed by the problems of others. You've also gotten out of the way so the appropriate person can come to aid. After establishing the habit of saying "yes" and "no" as appropriate, you've been successfully pulling out the bad roots and you can enjoy the peaceful view of a flourishing, well-boundaried yard.

I don't want to leave poor Wifey from earlier in this chapter in her cycle of problems. It seems wrong somehow, so I choose to help this fictional woman by giving her some suggestions regarding what steps she can take to help herself. Note that one of my suggestions isn't that I step in and fix him or the situation in any way. This is her life to deal with. If I step in and take it over (as if I even could, since this scenario is fictional!) I'm robbing her of the opportunity to have the success of solving her own problem. I'd be reinforcing her dependency on others to do so in the future. I'd be trampling through her yard. So, Miss Wifey, my suggestions are to build your own boundary by:

- Go to Al-Anon to strengthen your knowledge of alcoholism and the role you're playing in it
- Get counseling for yourself
- Get counseling for your kids, if age-appropriate
- Stop lying to your MIL, Mr./Ms.. Boss, and everyone else. Stop disrespecting your husband by taking away or hiding the thing that blocks people from seeing him as he truly is right now
- Demand better from him. Hand him the phone and tell him to call treatment facilities. Give him the timeline you feel comfortable with and stick to it!
- Learn to say "My husband had too much to drink so he's unable to ______________, but

the kids and I'll come to the party. What can I bring?"

- Stop enabling this evil in your home. This IS YOUR HOME, YOUR FAMILY, and you need to find a way to bounce Satan's giggling ass out the door! (Yes, I know that "ass" isn't usually acceptable Christian-ese, but it fits here. Saying "hind end" or "rear" makes it cleaner and cuter, and this is not a clean, cute situation. I don't like to make Satan giggle. Show him the curb.)
- Be prepared to separate from him, if necessary. Take the legal, safety and housing steps you must take if he refuses to get help.

Okay, you get the idea. Wifey has lots of options on her own. All these suggestions take his issue from her yard and put it right where it belongs, in his. Gate shut, lock set. His drunken dysfunction is now his to deal with, while her job is to protect her boundary with strength and appropriate pride so what grows in the yard for which she's created is healthy and beautiful.

CHAPTER 9-- BE A PERSON OF GOOD CHARACTER

This one should go without saying, right? To BE a right person for any type of relationship, we must have a strong, positive character or it's all off. So what is character, you ask? We often hear of "good character" or "bad character" or "a strange character," and so on, but what is it? Merriam-Websters' definition of character is "main or essential nature especially as strongly marked and serving to distinguish." Simply put, character refers to the inner qualities, traits and morals that distinguish you from others.

My mother had a quippy saying that "beauty is only skin deep but ugly goes all the way to the bone." That's a good way to look at character. It's how beautiful your 'bones' are. Not your actual ribs, ulnas or femurs, of course, but what lies beyond the outward appearance. Sadly, we can all probably think of politicians, celebrities or athletes who look great on the outside but a deeper look revealed they were not so great. Perhaps they were shown to be deceitful, untrustworthy, selfish or abusive. How many times have you seen an elected official who smiled broadly with his arm around his wife during the campaign only to discover that a girlfriend or two were also in that crowd? Or an athlete, admired for his discipline and skill on the playing court or field, is exposed by a video of his wife's bruises after his battering? These are unattractive, unacceptable bones. These stories go on and on and on but it never seems to quite make sense in our brains that people aren't always what they appear, We keep trusting people who smile at us, assure us of their trustworthiness as they sell us something that costs more than we can ever pay, financially, emotionally, and spiritually. These are people with bad character: an essentially deceitful and selfish nature.

Don't be a person with ugly 'bones.' Instead, choose to be a person who has respect and concern for others! Choose to hold up your head in any crowd, without furtively wondering if someone in the room knows your secret. Choose to be someone who wouldn't be embarrassed by your actions if caught on camera at any moment.

Take a good, honest look at your 'bones' and consider what you do when no one can see you. How do you treat people who might qualify as "the least of these" (Matthew 25:40), those people in society who have no political, financial or social power?

The mental picture of Matthew 25:40 has been my guiding force for my entire adult life. It is both lofty and attainable all at once. It calls for a constant and genuine love I do not possess but can easily ask to flow from me. It's an abandonment of self that, if done as an outpouring of the Spirit of God, moves every iota of preoccupation with self into the focus on another. This picture, to me, is a beautiful view of Jesus' perfect character of love, respect, dignity and truthfulness.

In my 30 plus years of working with severely mentally ill adults I've done some things right and royally messed up other things, but I hope with every cell that not one of the clients I've tried to serve will ever say "she was disrespectful of me" or "I couldn't depend on her. She'd blow me off like I didn't matter." Horribly, some of them could say such things. Perhaps they caught an eye-roll I didn't quite hide or they felt rushed in our conversation or unheard because I am so very busy and important (in my own mind only) and have other things to think about. Of course, I didn't 'click' with every client ever on my caseload, but hopefully I respected them with abandon, lifting up their dignity as Jesus would want me to do. This is what good character would look like in me. Since I'm a flawed human, like everyone is, the view is so much less beautiful than the picture we get from our Lord.

Never once in Scripture do we read of Jesus saying "Ewwww" when He was talking with a sick person who was sitting by the road for days on end, unbathed, unfed, unloved and powerless. Nor do we read of Him rushing to His next task with an air of haughty importance. Never do we read of Him dismissing someone or being untruthful or not being exactly Who He professed to be. Jesus' 'bones' are beautiful. His character is flawless.

What if you have a shady pattern in your character? While no human will ever have perfect character all the time like Jesus showed us, we can live a life that comes closer and closer to that ideal, but what if you haven't chosen to develop good character? Well, stop it. Just stop it now. Despite your place in life or how your parents, boss or 3rd grade teacher treated you, what you do for a living, your choice of faith, or anything else, you can choose to be a person of good character. Choosing to be trustworthy, honorable, dignified, kind and transparent in how you treat people is just that—a choice. Choose to practice good character until it becomes a firm habit. No one can do it but you, but you can certainly ask for help from a counselor, clergyperson, friend or anyone who will provide honest feedback and guidance.

There are many people in the pews on Sunday morning with good character —hopefully all of them. There are women you can confide in and trust that your words won't be gossip fodder. There are men who'll keep their promise to help you do some maintenance on your character. Will they get it right 100 percent of the time? Not likely, but they will choose to help you reach the goal of having Jesus-like character.

Without BEing a person of good character, the first six chapters of this book are useless. If you don't choose to be a person others can trust and feel honor in, it doesn't matter how you present yourself, how good you look, how you handle your money or anything else we've already discussed because your 'bones' will be ugly.

CHAPTER 10-- BE A PERSON WHO VALUES AND HOLDS SEXUAL INTEGRITY

Oh, boy! Here I am, at the beginning of the chapter I've so wanted to write for so long! I've tried to cement the value of sexual integrity into the heads of any and all single people I know because it's so critically important to life and, eventually, a happy, lasting relationship. Now that I'm here, though, I can see this stream I'll be going up is flowing extremely fast and may overwhelm me. I realize I'm becoming more and more a lone voice speaking against the culture we are in that encourages—possibly even demands—endless sexual involvements with endless sexual partners. I imagine some of you might be throwing this book across the room, or rolling your eyes as you read this chapter. (I KNOW my daughters are! Stop that!). You may think this topic is irrelevant today and we have "progressed" and I'm just ridiculous and out of touch with how things are. After all, "it's the 21st century." This is a direct quote I recently got regarding the subject. Sigh.

I dare you, if you're throwing or rolling, listen to my points with an open mind. See if anything I say might have some merit. I think you'll find yourself deeply considering some points.

I'll warn you, dear readers, in this chapter I may be more blunt than typical Christian-speak. Oh, I hope I am! I kind of gleefully hope some of you gasp with offended-ness at what I say. We need to speak very bluntly and clearly on this subject, do we not?

Before going any further, let's define some terms. What do I mean by "sexual integrity?" Look up the word "integrity." When I did, I found words like "moral," "upright" and "honest, even when no one is looking" and (my favorite) "behaving according to one's principles so as not to demean or dishonor oneself." Sexual integrity is the lifestyle of keeping sexual relations between a husband and wife in order not to dishonor or demean.

Okay, what am I calling "sexual interaction?" Is it only the big deed, the mattress dance, hiding the sausage, or whatever else intercourse might be called? (There really are some hilarious names for it, although some are pretty crude for such an amazing thing.) I don't think so although I suppose that could be what God means in 1 Thessalonians 4:3 when He says to "abstain from sexual immorality, that each of [us] will know how to possess [our] own vessel in sanctification and honor." I think the directive here includes any activity involving our tingly parts we wouldn't do in front of our grannies, our pastors, or law enforcement. Handholding at Nana's Sunday dinner will probably get you a sweet smile and maybe gentle teasing. The sounds of zippers coming down, however, probably wouldn't get so sweet a reaction. For our purposes, let's assume that sexual immorality involves anything that focuses on genitalia and eventual climax that's not happening between a married couple in private.

You, of the eye rolling and book throwing, may now be saying "And why do I want this sexual integrity thing, exactly? What good does it do for me to BE sexually honorable? How I'm living out my sexuality is fine. It's fun. No big deal." The answer is: Because you are worth more than what you think you are.

You're selling yourself short if you don't live with a high standard for your own sexual gloriousness. If you have no standard for your sexual behavior, you cheapen yourself—and the other person!-- time and time and time again, until you cannot even see it. If you don't understand "cheapen," keep reading. By the end of the chapter you'll get it.

Know What Sex Is and Is Not

So what the heck is it? Did you catch the beauty of verse 4 in 1Thessalonians 4 quoted above? We're to handle our sexuality with sanctification and honor. I love the honor part. Sex within marriage is honorable! It's a fun, over-the-top gift God gave us. He chose to give this special gift for the same reason He gave us strawberries, T-bone steaks, the wonderful smell of a carnation or anything else that's just so darn enjoyable that it must be a treat from a Creator who's totally in love with us! This gift is meant to be honored, which sets it aside from strawberries and carnations. Nowhere in Scripture I know of are we instructed regarding the possession of fruits or flowers bringing sanctification or honor. This is heavy stuff, that we're to treat ourselves and the matter of sexuality with honor and sanctification. Isn't it just like the perfect Creator to want this for us?

Unfortunately, isn't it just like our enemy to twist this beautiful gift of sex into something empty, horrid and almost soul-crushing? The mishandling of sex has caused unfathomable heartache. Broken relationships, broken trust because of affairs, the unthinkable selling and exploiting of our children, the trauma of rape and abuse, porn addicts not being able to pull themselves away from computer screens or images because the addiction to porn causes similar brain reactions as heroin, and feelings of inadequacy and emptiness and more are results of the mishandling. We now have a horrifyingly ugly picture of what was meant to be beautiful, but there are certainly ways of avoiding missteps.

Sex is an honorable gift, but it's been so distorted it's too rarely seen as such. We've listened to lies and been pulled away from the specialness of it. Our enemy gleefully uses this distortion to bring disharmony and pain so we miss the blessing we were meant to have. Let's look beyond the distortion and see what it is not.

- Sex does not equal love. Ohhhh, how I wish I and all women truly and fully understood that from Day One of our lives. Life would be so much simpler with so many less mistakes made and hearts broken. The act of intercourse and all it entails is designed to enhance love and specialness in a married relationship, but in and of itself it isn't synonymous with love. Remove all your romantic thoughts of any sexual contact and look at it for what it is. It's amazingly intricately designed as a release of hormones, physiological and psychological actions and reactions with more science-y things happening than I can understand or explain, but it is not in and of itself love. It's a biological action like eating. The digestive system does its job, just as the sexual/reproductive system does its job. Now, God does throw in the emotions, hormones, etc. that can sweeten and enhance sexual involvement, but there's nothing inherently loving and cementing about each and every sexual encounter. "Hooking up" with someone you meet one evening does NOT mean that he will automatically love you the following day. You aren't getting what you want.

- Unmarried sex isn't inherently an act of closeness, safety and intimacy. Quite the opposite. Think of it---in a sexual encounter, you make yourself completely vulnerable in multiple ways to another person who hasn't made any life commitments to you. They have zero tangible investment in you. During the time of the encounter, you're in a private place alone with this other person. Vulnerable, huge time. You've gotten naked and literally have no physical barriers between you and Person X. They're looking at your bumpy, scarred, tan-lined, too-big or not-big-enough, flabby-in-places, "I hate my butt" body which YOU live in, and you have no guarantee that they appreciate it and will keep your bodily secrets to themselves. WOW, amazing vulnerability! Then, once all the nakedness has been explored there's some kind of big finish. Women—you're allowing this man that has no commitment to you to invade your body, to actually insert part of his non-committing, non-invested self into you and do what he does until he puts stuff into you. He just leaves it there for you to deal with. Men—you're risking your pride, putting your beloved penis (oh, admit it—you guys all love your pee-pees! It was one of the things my three year old nephew thanked God for during his nightly prayers! You put a huge amount of importance on this organ!) into the body of someone who probably doesn't care that much about you, your dreams, thoughts or your core. You're literally giving part of you to her, and she has no real commitment to you! Then you are actually leaving a part of you in her,—and you have no say about what she does with it! She can literally grow a human being from what you've deposited in her, and make you pay for this human for 18 years. Or she could opt to have a human that's half you tossed away like last week's leftovers. Can you be any more vulnerable than this? And what do you have for your troubles at the end of the encounter? Sure, you've orgasmed, been complimented, maybe feel puffed up for a bit....until you don't, and you have to do it again. It's an empty occurrence that never produces the secure, safe connectedness you want. It seems intimate and profound but without the emotional connection and commitment it really is nothing. It's whorish, really You have traded your body for......what?

- Sex isn't proof of your manliness or womanliness. It just means that your body parts function, much like your lungs, eyes, vascular system or neural synapses do. Since you didn't design the parts and their functionality you cannot take credit for their performance. Yes, you can brag about it the next day, but think about what you're really bragging about---"Yeah, last night I found a stranger to get me to an orgasm. Heh, heh---how many people can do THAT?" Virtually everyone, dude. Literally almost every human being can go out and find someone who'll accept the illusion of "intimacy." No one with a brain is impressed because it's an empty "accomplishment."

- Sex does not fix your daddy issues, girls. If you're able to get any man you want to pursue you, want you, get him into your bed and literally pour himself into you, it still doesn't mean your dad loved you and you had a strong connection to him. There was only one chance for that, and if your dad didn't man up and be the father you deserved, that ship has sailed and it won't come back. You cannot replace your father, and you can't substitute any other relationship—even marriage—for the daddy/daughter relationship you were cheated out of.

I had to learn this the very hard way—with years (17, to be exact, off and on) of therapy. Before the lesson was cemented in my brain I traded my honor and sexual specialness too many times for….nothing. I was addicted to finding the "daddy" who would give me the affirmation, acceptance and honor I should've gotten from my real one and didn't. I went after "Targets," as I subconsciously called the men who seemed to best fit the bill. Can you imagine? I did the things we just talked about with real men that I barely thought of as human beings with feelings, needs of their own, etc. Oh, they went away happy, to be sure, because I 'proved my worth,' but they weren't real to me, not really. I didn't see them and I didn't require them to see me. They were Targets I used, thinking if I could draw them close enough and please them enough, they would surely say to me "Hey, Jill—your dad was wrong. He should've loved you." Funny thing....it never worked. It could not have worked. It's not possible for a substitution to work because there was one person tasked with that responsibility and he didn't do his part. If I had realized that truth in my teens, how much richer and more honorable my life have been would've been, and how much more I could've focused on more fun, deep and meaningful pursuits! Don't talk yourself into thinking that your experience will be different than mine, and all your needs will magically be met by someone else. Grieve the loss and hurt of what you didn't get from your father, and move past it.

- Likewise, sex isn't a substitute for the connection with your mom you so hungered for, guys. Did you know if a boy is separated from his mother between the ages of 10-14, he has a strong chance of becoming a sex addict? The separation could be any type of unplugging—an emotional separation, death, broken custody/visitation, or abandonment. He may grow into an adult who will bounce from one woman to another, never able to commit and never enjoying the depth of a relationship he could have with a wife. He is likely to use pornography as a facsimile for a real relationship. This is because at that pre-teen and young-teen age, boys developmentally learn how to navigate around the opposite sex. A boy must learn how to navigate and understand her emotions (HA!), her strengths and weaknesses, and respect and appreciate her general differentness from him. The mother/son relationship is where this development is supposed to happen because it's safe, guided and loving. Even if the separation wasn't purposeful on mom's part, it's indeed an interruption of the necessary developmental process. Consider former President Bill Clinton: his mother left him during his childhood years to do something quite honorable, educate and better herself. We all painfully know how that turned out! His Presidency and so much of the business of running the United States were interrupted by the distraction of his sex scandals. Clinton seems to have been an addict, trying to fill the huge hole in his heart and his maturity process but it just cannot be done. That ship has also sailed and the harbor is left bare. Sexual closeness can seem like a substitute for a close mom/son connection, but it isn't. It cannot be.

- Sex doesn't equal closeness. Real connectedness doesn't happen when a couple jumps into bed; it can't. Sex too early in a relationship forces it to a level of physical intimacy it's not ready for. In other words, instead of building a fabulous relationship of friendship, communication, respect, and sharing of hopes, dreams, regrets and goals, these critically important things are skipped entirely in favor of the pseudo-intimacy of having sex. Since sex is in fact greatly fun, the more important things are too often put to the side, in favor of a few moments of excitement and release. After a while, whatcha got? There may be memories of good sex, or there might not be. There won't be many memories of true closeness, real heart-to-heart conversations, shared tears, or anything else lasting. It's impossible to rewind to closeness-building conversations and moments after sex has been had too early, because the process of building intimacy is not reversible. It's impossible to really know and love someone based on seeing them naked and sexually involved. You'll have to fill in the blanks that were left when you jumped over them into bed, and you'll have only your fantasy of what you think the person is like. The truth of who a person is might be vastly different and one you might not like and shouldn't tolerate. Don't jump steps! Get the order of the process right the first time.

There are other reasons not to have multiple partners for this type of 'tango' other than honor and not falling prey to lies, such as:

- The more sex you have, the faster you're heading to the place in life where it will not be particularly heart-stoppingly enjoyable. All good things really do come to an end, even sex drives. The sexual activities you used to race toward become secondary to other life issues, as well they eventually should. Presuming there's fairly limited number of years that sex is awesome, why waste it? Wouldn't it be better to enjoy sex longer in your life rather than to burn out earlier? Let's face it, lasagna is an awesome food, and every cook makes it a little differently, but if you eat lasagna every night for 60 nights in a row, cooked by 30 different chefs, lasagna becomes much less exciting. (Note that I'm referring here to real lasagna, layered with pasta cheese and sauce. I'm not using some crude euphemism for sex. Although I suppose it's an interesting concept.) It wouldn't be very long into that 60 days when you'd watch the NBA game on TV rather than go through the effort of eating lasagna again, or you'd compare lasagna from Day 32 against lasagna from Day 41, and finding the 41-Day chef lacking. Different lasagnas may be tantalizing, to be sure, but wouldn't it be so much better to have one cook who knows exactly how you love your favorite meal and makes it exactly as you like it, and it's a special treat the two of you share? Let's be honest—sex doesn't really change much. Men have certain parts and women have certain parts and there's a limit as to what can be done with those parts. Really. If your goal is a lasting relationship, it's much more conducive to explore all the facets in the relationships. It will take you longer to explore them all, and it's a lot more fun!

- If the marriage bed is pure, that is, free from any sexual content other than what is between the wife and the husband, there's no risk of comparison. The husband never has to wonder whether his beloved wife is reminiscing back to another sexual experience, and the wife never has to wonder if she is being compared to other lovers. There's a great deal to be said for that. Having multiple partners in the rear window just means they're behind you, not non-existent, and never fully forgotten by either mate. You left those people behind for a reason. Why bring them into your bed now?
- There are risks to multiple-partner sex, and you know it. There's the risk of STD's, some of which cannot be easily antibiotic-ed away. Some diseases come with a life sentence, always a present and awful reminder of a bad decision. Some even come with a death sentence. Is a hay-roll really worth that risk? Is that how little you think of yourself? It's very difficult to explain any health issue to kids, such

as "Daddy has an STD." Why risk having to have that conversation in the future?

- Regardless of how "progressive" our culture has become or what year it is, people still look down upon a person who doesn't honor sex and has seemingly endless partners. Society still holds purity, self-control, honor, and respect as the ideal. Less than that is still looked down upon. If your eyes are rolling wildly in your head right now, consider words such as "skank", "womanizer", "slut." These are words often heard in reference to a person with a high number of sex partners who doesn't require respect for or to him or herself. Those or similar ones are meant in a negative, disparaging context. Why allow that kind of label to be the one people whisper about you? You can do much better.
- If you're always searching for your next conquest or hero and you always equate sex with the wrong thing, you miss out on a whole lotta life. You're focused only on the low-hanging fruit rather than going to the top of the

tree to harvest. The view from the top is much better, and the adventure of the climb is a lot more fun and a better challenge.

So, with these points in mind, do you understand why it just make sense for a better life and better readiness for a healthy, growing relationship to throw off the idea that sex is meant for casual fun and a good romp, like going to a football game? Sex with no commitment is just being used and you're better than that. You're being used –and you're using the other person—like a cat uses a toy. It's a brief distraction and amusement, then it's discarded. You are created for much more than that. You're NOT a worthless nothing that must beg for every scrap of love or its facsimile you can possibly get, in any form which someone else calls love.

If I allow myself to be treated like a cat toy, I've surely cheapened myself, have I not? If I don't see my body and emotions as extremely valuable, I cannot expect anyone else to do so. I'm actually volunteering to be devalued. Likewise, if I don't see another person's body and emotions as at least equally valuable I'm demeaning them. By dishonoring both myself and my partner I'm screaming from the mountain top that I'm just not ready for a lasting relationship. I have a lot more work to do.

Take a moment and write out (or draw or collage or whatever you want to do) how you have valued sex up to now. Even if you haven't had unmarried sex (YAY! Good for you!! Sooo proud of you!), put into words your feelings and thoughts about your sexual value. How do you look at sex, and why? Who taught you? What have you done or not done in this area that's made you proud? Do you have regrets? How do you think a sexual partner--he who has given an important part of himself to your body, or she who has accepted you into the depths of her body--deserves to be treated? How do YOU deserve to be treated? What are you volunteering for?

SEX VALUES

PART I-- CONCLUSION

Now that you've completed Part 1, you're a perfect person, right? HAHAHAHAHA—kidding!! Never for a minute do I believe this book, Divinely inspired though it is, can produce such wondrous results. We won't be perfect or even perfectly prepared for relationships as long as we draw breath on this earth. We simply won't achieve that level of greatness. What we can hope to accomplish is a surge of progress toward the goal of preparedness. Hopefully if you've worked your way through Part 1 you're more aware of yourself, what you want, what you need to strive toward, and what you need to leave behind in a stinky heap to be strong, healthy and honest enough to build a relationship of worth.

So how do you feel so far? Do you feel like you're making progress? Have you made changes, or confirmed that you're the person you want to be?

I may have missed something important to you. Take a few minutes to think about anything you want to add. Consider anything you believe is important to you BEing a person ready for a great relationship. You won't hurt my feelings one bit by adding a few things. It's important for you to grasp everything you want to grasp. YOU are important! Never doubt that truth!

NOTES ON PART 1

PART II-- FIND THE RIGHT PERSON

Hooray! We've made it this far! I hope that you've thought a lot, giggled a bit, seen some surprises, maybe even been offended, and have made notes in your journal that give you a much better idea of who you are, how you present yourself, and how to self-respect enough to stay on top of all aspects of health, money and " baggage." That's a lot to take in and ponder. If you haven't thought, giggled, been surprised or offended, or made notes then one of two things needs to happen:

- Re-read the entire Part 1. Use a highlighter this time.
- Put the book in your "Donate" pile and I need to move away from my computer

Assuming you're still reading and in fact are eager for Part II, here we go....

PART II is like PART I in that it talks about a healthy, functioning, vibrant person who's ready and able to give the best of himself/herself. The difference is, of course, the change in perspective. We're going from a first-person perspective to a third person one.

Our first-person perspective said, for instance, "I want to present better" or "I want to think about some things I might need to change" and we change to "She will have to be a person of very good character before I'll choose to have a relationship with her" or "He needs to be more self-aware before it would be safe to enter into a relationship with him." Basically, we're going to re-visit PART I from a perspective of potential buyer as opposed to potential seller. No, no, no—of course I'm not speaking of actual buying or selling of people, that's beyond evil and ridiculous; please try to get my drift here. I'm talking about the "product" you confirmed or obtained or improved in PART I---you! You, ready for a healthy, vibrant, and fulfilling relationship! PART II deals with the "product" that someone else has been working on, and you making a good choice regarding all the "products" you could choose.

It seems an ideal time to ask the question WHY. WHY do you want to find a right person for a relationship? Give that some very honest thought. Are you looking for companionship and someone to share your events, dreams, thoughts, aspirations, etc with? Or do you feel like you absolutely must have someone at your side? How do you feel about being alone? What does 'alone' mean to you? Does it mean 'loser,' 'undesirable,' 'unvaluable', etc? Substitute a word for 'alone' in this sentence, "I want to find someone for a relationship so that I won't be alone." Think about the word you put in there—does it seem like a healthy, vibrant reason to search for a person for a relationship, or do you have more work to do?

We've all known or known of people who tether themselves to someone, ANYone, just so they won't be alone. Guess what---they're likely to be more alone than they started out if they choose badly out of desperation. If we start the searching process with a feeling of "I've got to find someone or I will not be ok" we may be doomed

I have never understood how some people can detest or fear being alone so much that they will glue themselves to anyone who comes along because they came along. There's great blessing in being alone. I LOVE aloneness—being able to do anything or go anywhere without having to consider another's feelings or input is extremely enticing to me. The fact of not having to mind my manners all the time is exhilaratingly freeing! Marriage or friendship certainly is a valued blessing, but oh the joy of being able to scratch anywhere at any time, play my music or TV show as softly or as loudly as I want, talk to myself while doing an enjoyable activity or simply sit in absolute silence and peace is a time of great bliss. Until it isn't. It's only good until I get bored of my own company and want the connection to another human being that I was designed to want.

In the story of God's creation of man and woman, God commented that it isn't good for man to be alone. Sometimes I think that means that specifically a MAN should not be alone because he needs help finding the mayonnaise in the fridge in the spot where it has been kept since the refrigerator was purchased, or other simple task that men seem to need lots of help with, but that thought's really neither here nor there. God designed us to need others. It wasn't good for Adam to hang out by himself because it is much harder to laugh alone or enjoy Creation's beauty by oneself, and we cannot usually kiss our own boo-boos, and of course there's the whole "populate the Earth" thing.

Like it or not, we need people. We need people at a superficial level like co-workers, people in line with us at the pharmacy, and so forth, but we also need much deeper connections. It is certainly possible to live a full and rewarding, contributing life without a mate, but deep connections are necessary. We don't know how long it was between when God made Adam and when He made Eve, but I think it's safe to assume that Adam existed quite sufficiently without Eve. He breathed, ate, laughed, frolicked, maybe made armpit noises, and did whatever one would do in a garden of perfection. But a lack was noticed and remedied, and Eve was brought alongside Adam.

The question really is "Am I wanting a relationship because I feel incomplete without someone?" You're not un-whole if you're not in a dating relationship. You're a whole person, no matter what. You're who God created you to be. You aren't missing any parts you were supposed to have, so don't put anyone in a space that isn't there. A healthy perspective of the desire to find someone is one of "I am living my life, with God's help, to the best of my ability and it is good and full of accomplishments and creations, but I do need and want someone to come along side me and be a 'helper' to me as I live this life, like God said Adam needed, but I'm okay even if I never find that person. It is enough to live life with God and close friends and I do NOT have to fill a spot that I think is empty, because I am not looking to complete what He has already completed." The goal should be to add to your life, not find a person you think will magically complete it. No one can do that and having that goal will just lead you to despair. Give a lot of deep thought to your answer to the question of WHY you want a relationship. The answer could change your perspective on a lot of things!

CHAPTER 11-- **FIND A PERSON THAT YOU ARE NOT "SETTLING FOR"**

You do not have to "settle" for a person who isn't a good choice for you, and that person does not have to be the "settled for" one. You—and the other person—are worth far more than that and were created for far more than that. Roll that sentence around in your mind until it sounds solid. For some of you, that will be one roll around, but for others it may take a few dozen or hundred rolls around.

The story of Leah (Genesis, Chapters 29 and 30) is probably the saddest love story ever. Please read it, from Leah's perspective. In a nutshell, Leah is forced to be the "settled for" one because her father tricks her future husband, Jacob, into marrying her instead of her sister Rachel who Jacob really loves. Jacob marries Leah first, then must to work for seven years to "earn" Rachel. Leah is the older sister and she has "weak eyes" we're told in verse 17. It isn't clear what that exactly means, but apparently it's not a good thing because the next part of the verse says, "but Rachel was beautiful." Some commentaries note that 'Leah' means “weary”, so maybe Leah’s eyes had no sparkle or twinkle, and she was sad-eyed and downcast. Perhaps she was sight-impaired. Whatever the case may be, Leah wasn’t a boyfriend magnet; she, as the older daughter, should’ve been married before this story begins but she isn’t and her father feels it necessary to take action himself to marry this girl off and resorts to trickery to do so. She is handed off as a substitute for the one that’s genuinely desired.

Can you imagine Leah’s pain? She has lived for many years knowing that she isn’t deemed beautiful in form and face like her sister, because of a weakness of some sort over which she had no control, then she learns she is engaged but must hide her identity because she knows that her intended wants someone else! In fact, she knows as Jacob “goes into” her on their wedding evening, that his passion and love and adoring words are for her sister, not her. I can’t imagine her devastation and mortification the next morning as she sees her husband’s expression when he realizes it is Leah, or as she watches him stomp off to complain to the tricking father. It makes my heart hurt.

Jacob eventually marries Rachel also—there's a fun family environment! The two women spend several years trying to out-birth the other. Each sister tries to give Jacob more sons than the other one does. Rachel does this out of jealousy toward Leah but poor Leah, cranks out baby after baby in the desperate hope that "Surely now my husband will love me" (back to Chapter 29). That's going to extremes to "get" someone's love. Does this strategy work for Leah? No, apparently it doesn't because we're told that Leah repeatedly says, "NOW my husband will love/become attached to me," and that when Rachel dies Jacob builds a pillar over her but when Leah dies he simply buries her in the family cave. Now, maybe being buried in the family burial cave (eww!) is a sign of honor or something. I don't know, but what strikes me is that there's no mention of Jacob being sad enough that she is gone to build any type of structure in her honor. Leah was the one he had to "settle for," nothing more.

How awful a situation, for all concerned! We see Leah is filled with great despair and futile hope, Rachel is jealous and scheming, and Jacob.....? Well, yeah,

Jacob seems to get LOTS of sex (there are maids involved, too, so he's a busy boy) but he lives in a contentious household and his deep love for Rachel hits some angry snags. A settled-for situation wasn't in anyone's best interests. All because Jacob had to settle for Leah, and she had to be the settled-for one.

While no one person can always meet every criteria you may have or dream of having for a partner in a relationship, you shouldn't have that sinking feeling in your heart of, "Oh, well. I guess this is the best I can do so I'll make do." No! God doesn't want you to "make do"—He wants you to live an abundant life, remember? (John 10:10) Abundance doesn't imply that you take the first person who comes along or the last one in a string of broken relationships because you think there will be no other choices. The very word, abundant, means an overflowing of plenty, of fullness. If you settle for something you know in your heart isn't the best relationship for you, it's like you are volunteering to give up the idea of fullness and abundance. Don't do that. Volunteering for misery and disappointment isn't the good way to go.

With abundance there's no sense or feeling of incompleteness, emptiness or lack. It's a heart overflowing with love, joy, trust and security, with no room for thoughts of "Gee, I wanted more" or "I think the neighbor over there looks better for me." So often we grab something that's full of 'lack' and miss out on the "abundance" because we think something is better than nothing. Often we aren't patient enough to wait for the good something or someone to come along. We lie to ourselves and convince ourselves a certain person is the answer to our need for abundance, when they're in fact lack with a capital L! Stop it! Just stop. Again, no one person can meet all your needs all the time, but there shouldn't be a prevailing feeling of lack in your relationship. Thoughts of regret over your choice or grief over what you have missed out on shouldn't be what you carry with you every day.

So how do you know who will bring abundance to your life? This requires much honest thought, my reading friend. Just as you made lists in PART 1, I encourage you to make a list of your requirements in a relationship partner, to clarify your thinking as well as provide a template you can refer to in the future.

Make a list including you Absolute Musts as well as your Preferences, as there are some things that are more important than others. Realistically, no one will match your entire list 100 percent but it is very important they match the Absolute Musts to that degree, and many of the Preferences are met.

Before meeting my current husband, I made such a list. I had over 40 items on it, including he'd be a committed Christian, have no serious prison record, have many friendships over 10 years old, have salt-and-pepper hair, be between 40-45 years of age, be good with computers, either have no children or have grown ones, have a solid work history in a career he enjoys and purposely chose, have a great sense of humor, be very intelligent, etc. etc. Making my list was, truly, one of the smartest things I ever did. I took the time to really think about what I wanted. I didn't think about what I thought I deserved or who I might talk into wanting me or who my family/friends would approve. Instead I considered but the traits I required to have the best chance of building and maintaining a successful—abundant!—relationship. I held fast to my list, rarely adding to it and NEVER deleting an item from it. This list was a guiding force for me as I dated; if someone didn't meet the Absolute Musts and many of the Preferences I moved on. I didn't talk myself into settling for someone who didn't meet the minimum requirements of my well-thought out, black-and-white list, as I probably would've if I didn't have a tangible list I set for myself. I had to trust myself and my judgment; I had to trust myself to have created a list worthy of sticking to, even while having some dates with men that "probably would do." I had to let go of in-the-moment emotions in favor of sticking to the blueprint I crafted for myself.

I'm delighted and proud to say that my husband, though not perfect, met over 90 percent of the requirements I put on my list! Though far from easy, our marriage since 1999 has been one based on choice and not settling for anything. Our love and appreciation for each other grows daily. I heartily recommend make a list and stick to it: craft a good blueprint for yourself and commit to trusting it!

As in your other lists, be very honest with this one. Be specific, with measurable items so you can't wiggle and adjust your list to fit a specific person. No one else gets to judge this list, so go for broke. List out every single thing you require in a significant other. Slowly and carefully list your requirements/desires for a person who will hold a significant place in your life. Go big, when it comes to issues of faith and character. Go little, when it comes to issues like hair and eye color. Think of everything! Review Part 1 of this book-- since you've had to work so hard to get through Part 1, it is only fair and right you find someone who has also done the difficult work on their honest self awareness, presentation, baggage, and money management and so on. Consider what you want those things to look like in a relationship partner. Here are some suggestions to get you started:

- What faith will a good match have?
- How they will they live out that faith?
- Age preference
- Career path. What color "collar" best suits you?
- Whether they have children or not
- How they feel about animals
- Where they want to live
- How many long friendships they have

- Number of exes
- Habits

Your list should include several dozen attributes. Be as comprehensive as you can be, listing everything important to you.

You can adjust your list as you learn and evaluate further, but it should remain fairly firm in most areas. Think of it like our American Constitution; the Constitution gets amended from time to time, but the basic gist is written IN STONE. Likewise, a good list of requirements for a relationship partner should be written with almost no wiggle room, so you can't adjust the list to fit the person. Remember, the person must fit your list, not the list fitting the person! In other words, if you meet a person who says nice things to you but hasn't held a job in over 20 years, has only friends who are drinking buddies, still lives with the parents yet talks very hatefully about them, or uses the term "Restraining Order" regularly in conversations, you canNOT adjust your list to fit this person. Don't give one second of energy into making this person fit your list—he or she isn't the one for you! Trust yourself and your list, Move on from anyone who doesn't meet most of the requirements you've stated for yourself.

Once you've made a list of your requirements and preferences, let it roll around in your head for a few days or weeks. Evaluate it to be sure you haven't left anything out, you've been fair and kind to yourself, and boldly honest about what you want. This isn't being judgmental! You're not judging a person, you're simply listing the traits that appeal to you. The following chapters in PART 2 will help you be sure you've included all important items on your list so you're positioned in the strongest, healthiest way.

You might be wondering where love falls in this listing business? It doesn't. Not yet. Yes, you must have

that in-love feeling that will mature into a deeper love, but for now your purpose is looking honestly at who to

even consider making a candidate for your affections. It's possible to convince yourself you're in love with or have sparks toward a lot of people. My goal is to help you become more aware and stronger in yourself so you can make the best decision regarding who to choose. The falling-in-love part is up to you. It’s certainly important, but it’s unwise to skip over all the other things we’re discussing to get to it. Or, worse yet, to claim “in love” status if you haven’t done the work to make that meaningful.

REQUIREMENTS LIST	
ABSOLUTE MUSTS	REALLY PREFER

CHAPTER 12-- FIND A PERSON WITH NO DEAL-BREAKERS!!

There's currently a word I find quite silly and even disgusting---"judgy". Current culture says we should never ever judge a person or their actions because everything is to be celebrated and embraced. Baloney! Even stronger— horse poopie!! That thinking, though kind and accepting on the surface, is ridiculous. We MUST judge behaviors and we do it all the time. It is how we stay alive. I'm not referring to judging based on skin color, background, parents' income, intelligence level, and other things that are beyond a person's control. Nor am I suggesting shunning or shaming anyone. I'm talking about evaluating a person's behavior in order to determine if they're safe, a good match for us, and have potential for a long, healthy relationship.

There are, my friends, people in the world who as a life pattern do bad things and therefore are not worthy of being chosen to be a significant part of our lives while they engage in the harmful behaviors and patterns. Am I saying that we are to judge someone's actual worth? Of course not! The Bible tells us over and over to love every person with a genuine affection, but we are also told to recognize foolish behavior and to "...be on the alert" to avoid being devoured (1 Peter 5:8). Certainly, there's a vast difference between a person and their behavior. However, we must be willing to see harmful behavior patterns for what they are: harmful and therefore to be avoided. God creates each person, so we all have infinite worth since we're created by His hand and breath, but many people choose not to live up to this value. Instead, they make harmful choices out of their own past hurts or a depraved need to control and overpower others. It's okay to not let a person who's harmful have a lot of space, time, energy, or money in our lives. It's not okay for us, our family, or even for the hurtful person to allow evilness to continue.

I once told a group of co-workers I was proud of one of my daughters who had decided not to spend a lot of time with a friend who was doing drugs, having sex (she was in middle school!), skipping school, etc. Those are very poor choices and probably made as a result of a sad home life, and I felt horrible for the girl and would've loved to help her value herself enough to make healthier choices, but the bottom line is she was in fact making those bad choices. I was very happy that my daughter could see that spending a great deal of time with her would not be healthy or positive in the long run. In fact, it could actually be dangerous. A very sweet co-worker known to embrace every person's every choice as sacred, said, "That seems very judgmental to me." I thanked her. I told the group I believe embracing every lame-brain decision someone makes is a silly and dangerous way to live, and that I was very proud of my girl for her choice to spend most of her time with healthy, forward-moving people. My daughter did not judge the person's value; she simply chose to not risk any splash-back on herself from the girl's poor choices. To this day I can't for the life of me understand how determining who is and is not a good choice to spend our time with is a bad thing…'judgy'. Recognizing if someone is spiraling in harmful ways and then creating safe boundaries with that person is necessary and wise. It has nothing to do with placing a value on the person.

So, what are deal-breaking behavior patterns? I mean behaviors that cannot and must not be tolerated, enabled, ignored, hidden under the carpet, excused and allowed to bring destruction and harm to your life if you're truly to find the right person for a relationship. Everyone has triggers or soft spots that are especially hurtful to us, and Lord knows there's virtually no end to the list of flaws humans have, but there are a few behaviors that universally should NEVER be invited into our lives or allowed to stay.

ABUSE

This one is a no-brainer. Obviously, no human being should live with abuse inflicted by another person. Never. Nope. No one has the right to say hurtful things to you, slap or punch you, choke you, control you, pinch you, violate you sexually, or in any other way harm you. Nor do you EVER have the right to do such things to another person. We all know this is unacceptable, right? Surely in this day and age we've overcome tolerance of abuse, right? Sadly, no. Abuse is rampant in our society and there's plenty of proof, in the numbers of domestic violence services, child abuse hotlines and agencies, counselors who specialize in abuse and trauma recovery, news articles, TV shows, and on and on and on. We're all painfully aware that too many people hurt too many other people.

Yet, so many people "settle for" an abuser. If this describes you, please, please, please commit to changing that pattern! Find a counselor, read books, talk with a clergyperson, call a hotline or even a talk show, ANYTHING to break the pattern of believing you're only good as a punching bag or an object to be abused. You're worth infinitely more than that! Stop excusing the behavior---you don't deserve it and it didn't happen because he or she had a bad day, was tired, the kids were loud, they lost their job, etc. No, the abuser chose to abuse. You were hit because someone thinks it is okay to put their fist on your face, push you into a wall or kick your ribs after knocking you onto the floor. You were called that awful name because someone thinks it's okay to throw vileness at you. It's not. It is destructive and it is evil. You do not deserve it ever, for any reason. Stop excusing this devouring lion. There are ways out—find one. Today. This hour.

The first step to avoiding being an abuse victim is to call the behavior what it is. Don't be drawn to "strength" when it is really bullying. Don't continue to tolerate "love taps" or "discipline" because they are neither—they're assaults. The barbs aren't "kidding" and they are not funny nor are they meant to be. Mean words are meant to belittle and disable; they are abuse. The abuser doesn't "want you so much, baby, that I lost my head", they're forcing sexual contact on you. Listen to your friends when they tell you the person you're dating or considering dating gives them the creeps. There's a reason they're telling you this. Hear them.

Literally for Christ's sake, do NOT continue in a relationship with someone you have or have even considered putting a Restraining Order on. I'm not using Jesus' name disrespectfully here—I mean for you to break off any relationship with a violent person for the glory and honor of Christ! It doesn't glorify God if you stay with an abuser to "help" him, or to "rescue" her or to be "submissive." God in fact tells us NOT to enable this (or any) evil! In Proverbs 10:10 we're told that if we "wink our eye we cause trouble" and in

Proverbs 16:30 that if we "compress our lips we bring evil to pass." (I've paraphrased here, changing the pronouns to fit my point, but the meaning is the same.) Looking the other way or keeping our mouths shut when evil is happening is never being Godly, but it is especially true when dealing with abuse. I believe it breaks God's heart and maybe even embarrasses Him a bit when a person He loves continues to allow herself/himself to be abused. It's not what He created us for!

Recently I was told of a dear friend's niece who has stayed with a physically and emotionally abusive man for over 20 years, after a very rocky dating relationship which included at one point a restraining order to protect her from his violence. Huge red flag, my reading friends. Run far and run fast when a safety plan of any type must be made! She is an amazingly talented, beautiful and smart young woman, but she accepts harmful behavior and doesn't call it what it is. Within a few months of the restraining order being issued she became pregnant by him. They got married without doing any of the work necessary to remove his unhealthy and hurtful actions from the relationship.

She's stayed with this still-controlling man (who, by the way, professes Christ as his Savior. Sheesh) because she wants to be a "submissive" wife as the Bible directs (Eph. 5:22) but she is missing the whole point. Her role as a wife isn't described in one verse only. She needs to read more of God's instruction book to find the life He planned for her.

Guess how this "submitting" without requiring change is working out for her? Not well. Although he may basically be a well-meaning man with lots of good characteristics deep down, she's had to leave him numerous times because of his drinking and abuse, has to deal with his multiple ex-wives/girlfriends and the kids he's had with them (another red flag!!) and watches him belittle their adorable children, all because she thought it is honorable to wink and compress. She's wrong. Staying in this abusive relationship has devastated her life, crippled her children's entire childhoods and probably their lives. It has also allowed her husband to continue in his evil selfishness of not getting the help he needs. No one has held him accountable for colluding with the Enemy. This wife has upheld and honored that which is not honorable. What is glorifying about that? I don't think God smiles broadly when a victim chooses to stay in an abusive situation; I believe He is deeply grieved in His heart to see this devastation continue. Imagine the joy and pride that's possible if this wonderful woman took a stand, stopped enabling the behavior and took the bold move of demanding her husband become the safe, nurturing, healthy man he should be to lead their family!

Don't stay trapped in a hamster-wheel of abuse then apologies then abuse then apologies...... The wheel will only stop turning when the hamster gets off it. Be a strong hamster! Find your power, stop enabling, and walk away to something much better.

CHEATING

Find a person who has zero tolerance for cheating and has zero—ZERO-- history of cheating. You cannot and should not trust a person who doesn't behave in ways that are trustworthy, especially in the early stages of a relationship when most people put their best foot forward. If someone hides their phone or email from you they're most likely doing something they really don't want you to know about. There's no room for such behavior in a healthy relationship. Unless they have a valid reason such as client confidentiality or HIPAA restrictions, or are a secret agent for the CIA (verify this. Make them show you a paycheck stub!) you ought to be able to glance at their phone or texts at any time. You probably shouldn't answer their phone, texts or emails because that's quite intrusive and rude, but the atmosphere of your relationship ought to be open and honest, with nothing hidden. If there's an air of secrecy or defensiveness or if you just have a gut feeling that's not put to rest by conversations with the other person, you probably haven't found the right person. Walk away.

Someone with has a history of cheating on a partner isn't likely to have "changed" unless they've done an enormous amount of work on the deepest parts of their heart. Don't believe someone who says they've changed without earning the right to say it. You cannot change them. You'll never be able to love him enough to make him stay faithful to you if he is a habitual cheater. You can never love her enough to make her become someone with sexual integrity if she has a bad track record. Don't settle for someone you have to lie to yourself about!

Many women and, increasingly many men, face the betrayal of a partner due to an addiction to pornography. This can be every bit as painful as a flesh-and-blood affair. A person addicted to pornographic material can become isolative, cutting off his/her spouse in favor of the "perfect" image they're looking at. This image never asks him to take out the garbage or criticizes her or anything else a real person might do. Real people equal real life. Air-brushed images or lurid stories equal fantasy life. They create an ideal no one can live up to, cheapening the real person the addict married. There's growing evidence addiction to porn changes the brain much like heroin does. There's the rush of adrenaline, the enjoyment, and it's all totally self-absorbing. No one requires anything else from you during an experience with porn. It's all about you and your pleasure. That might sound just fine, but damage has been done. It's now more difficult to deal with your real-life mate because they aren't always ready-to-rumble at your whim nor do they require anything from you. Your mate may feel second-best or overlooked and that's a hurt which is hard to overcome.

An excellent resource on this issue is Every Man's Battle by Stephen Arterburn and Fred Stoker and the counterpart book is Every Woman's Battle by Shannon Ethridge. Both fully discuss the impact of porn addiction and provide strategies and help getting free of it. If porn is affecting you, take a look at these resources. Begin your healing.

ADDICTIONS

We all give our lives over to something. Perhaps we lead our lives driven by selfishness, or duty or wind-chasing of one type or another, etc. Hopefully we let our lives be ruled by God's Spirit, serving Him in the way He leads and walking with Him in the adventures He wants us to walk through. Additionally, a mature and healthy person runs life based on responsibilities, commitments, integrity, openness, balance, excellence on the job, creativity, and general reliability. Gee, that sounds potentially very dull and joyless, doesn't it? I stand by it, though—we can certainly live lives with joy, laughter, love, silliness, playfulness, and adventurousness but we must live lives based on the patterns I've listed here to be stable people who are ready for a relationship. We must be able and willing to make decisions and life choices based on these patterns, not patterns brought on by the chaos of an addiction to something harmful.

A person who doesn't live life by these mature attributes may instead have given her/his life over to something that's harmful to all in its path. It's not a surprise, I'm sure, to hear that someone who's addicted to alcohol, drugs, gambling, shopping, overeating, pornography, weight loss, or any of the other virtually endless items one can be addicted to, can be controlled by their need for their item of choice. All real choice goes flapping merrily out the window; they have given their lives over to the item of addiction and all decisions and actions revolve around it.

Finding the right person requires open eyes and an honest mind. You must be aware of what is critically important to a person you're interested in forming a relationship with, beyond lip service. Many times addicts will live two lives: the one they want to live and the darker one they're really living. To be sure to find the right person you must be willing to look beyond the smiles, flirtations, nice dates, appearance, etc. to see what is really driving the person. What has control of the other person's life? What does he spend most of his free time doing? What does she spend most of her money on? Is the tv or computer always on something that anyone can see, or does it get hastily shut down when you or a child or great-gramma walks into the room? You must be willing to find and face facts in order to have a complete picture of whether a person is the right one for a relationship. If it seems that he shouldn't be drinking so much, he probably shouldn't be drinking so much. If it seems like she shops a great deal and many of the clothes in her closet still have tags on them, she is probably shopping too much.

As with abuse and cheating, you must NOT close your eyes to the truth of the harmfulness of an addiction. You shouldn't excuse it or re-name it or put blame where it doesn't belong. Someone who's an active addict isn't living their own life but is letting the addiction live in their body, and that can never be a workable facet in a relationship. A relationship where one person is the enabler and the other is the addict might limp along for a while but has no abundance of the blessings a good relationship has.

UNTREATED MENTAL HEALTH INSTABILITY

We probably all can agree that we're all mentally unhealthy from time to time. Everyone gets depressed sometimes, everyone has anger issues on—hopefully! —rare occasions, or binges on something for a time but most of us can pull out of these issues and go on with a productive, loving life. Sometimes, though, pulling out of the issue isn't possible on our own. When a person's actual brain chemistry is out of whack due to a thought or mood disorder or addiction, outside help is needed to get it running smoothly again. Until that's completed, a person isn't ready for a healthy relationship.

The key phrase here is "untreated." If someone has been diagnosed as bi-polar and they faithfully take the prescribed meds, alert their doctor of any changes or symptoms, etc., that's a treated disorder, and the person is managing it responsibly and healthily and this isn't a deal-breaker any more than diabetes would be. If, however, a person has been diagnosed as having

Major Depression but does not follow a prescribed treatment, refuses meds or counseling, stays in bed for weeks at a time, has trouble maintaining employment and has not left the house in over a year, this is a deal-breaker. This person isn't healthy, period, let alone healthy enough for a relationship with another person.

Let's really think about what is acceptable and what is a deal breaker. Is a little clutter acceptable? Probably. How about an all-out hoarder? Probably not: there are deep issues of fear and abandonment and compulsion that must be resolved in a hoarding situation and until those are dealt with the person is probably not ready. What about someone who thought about suicide when she was 14? Probably, assuming there are no attempts or ideations since then and she's worked with a counselor. But what if it was just a couple of months ago, and that last attempt was #23 in a long history? Much less acceptable, right?

The issue of mental health being a deal breaker or not really comes down to the sufferer's attitude about their diagnosis and their willingness to get treatment. While not all treatments work for all patients, a person MUST be open to seeking treatment until the right one is found. Denial of an illness when evidence points otherwise and refusal to get necessary treatment fall into the deal breaker category because there will not be two healthy people in this relationship; there will be one caretaker pulled into the sickness and one sick controller.

Are people who have these deal-breaking behaviors evil or worthless? No. Again, as humans made by the Hand and Breath of God, everyone has immeasurable worth and value. But certain behaviors should be avoided.

It isn't romantic to try to "rescue" an abuser, addict etc. It is foolish and, frankly, pathetic. You cannot love him or her enough to erase all the anger and entitlement the abuser feels. Sweet cards, over-apologizing, romantic evenings and hand-and-foot waiting on will not correct the misfiring of the brain. That will accomplish, most likely, just the opposite—you'll set up a situation that enables the abusive or addictive behaviors or illness to thrive. You can do better --and so can the abuser. Don't enable the bad behavior—stand against it, require change!

In summary of Chapter 12, be wise, open your eyes and never, ever cry over the same person and same behavior twice. The old saying "Fool me once, shame on you. Fool me twice shame on me" holds true today. The first time a deal-breaker—any type of abuse or cheating or out-of-control behavior--smacks you upside your head is on the smacker. Once the 'smacking' history is established, subsequent smacks are all on the "smackee"— you. Don't accept it. Don't volunteer for more bad behavior. EVER. You can do better. You need to pray that your wonderful Creator will show you that you are worth more, and you may need help from a counselor, but you can and must do better than to accept deal-breaking behavior.

CHAPTER 13-- FIND A PERSON WHO HAS READ AND MASTERED—PART 1 OF THIS BOOK

Now that we've talked about the definite no-no's of who to choose, let's look at who is a good choice. Maybe someone who's a great choice has read this book too. Super! Another sale for me, and a great topic of many discussions for you! Win/win!

This is a good time to re-look at your list of requirements of a relationship partner and review Part 1 with your list in mind. Compare the two. Remember, your list can be added to from time to time, but very rarely subtracted from! This list isn't to the IN STONE phase until you've honestly decided that you're healthily ready for a relationship and are ready to step out into the dating/social world. Once you make that decision, the list is pretty much IN STONE, to protect you from making adjustments to fit the latest person to cross your path instead of making the list work for you as a strong guide to getting who and what you want. So, look at your requirements list and make sure it covers the issues in Part 1 that are important to you and you require in a mate or friend.

What did you learn about your requirements? What from Part 1 is most important to you? What traits did you put in the Absolute Musts column, and which did you put in the Preferences column?

Well, this chapter was quick and easy for me to write! It should not have been quick or easy for you to work through. If it was, you missed the point and need to re-do.

The point of this chapter is to make sure that, just as you worked to make yourself as healthy and presentable as possible, you have a strong blueprint to find someone who's also as healthy and as issue-free as possible. No one is 100 percent perfect 100 percent of the time, but the ideal person to FIND for a relationship is one who's moving toward good goals.

CHAPTER 14-- FIND A PERSON WHO HAS STRENGTHS YOU LOVE AND ISSUES YOU CAN DEAL WITH

You might be thinking "um, she is getting loony in that title---wouldn't I love someone's strengths? Isn't that the basic definition of a strength—something admirable and inspiring?" Well, good catch but I disagree. There are many wonderful strengths that talented, strong, mature, and healthy people have that I personally would HATE to have around me 24/7. For instance, someone who can create beautiful works of art like paintings or drawings maybe wouldn't be someone that would be a good person for me to find for a relationship because I have zero artistic talent and therefore little knowledge or interest in art. I'd rather be on the couch making armpit noises if the mood struck me to do so. I personally would feel bad about my horrid lack of artistic talent, and I could never understand the person's thinking or fit into the time commitment they would need to work on their talent. Plus, I want a logical, rational-thinking person and an artist probably thinks in more beautiful, creative, and open terms than that. Likewise, I wouldn't want to find a person for a close relationship who's a star athlete or musician; it just seems to me that their talent would absorb my limited talent and understanding of music or sports and swallow me up. I don't want to live in someone's shadow all the time, and I'd be resistive and defensive.

These two examples might be rather lame, as there are many variables and moving parts in those scenarios, but I'm pretty darn confident that I could not have a close relationship with a teacher. Though I see the vast pricelessness of the teaching profession, teachers can often bug me. There, I said it. Give me a moment to take in a breath after that rather daring statement. Ok. Teachers must be scheduled, organized and somewhat rigid in their thinking and planning, and social workers (like me) cannot be those things. Because teachers must get certain things accomplished, they require a routine and order. Because social workers usually work with people who have special needs of some sort, we absolutely can't be rigid or expect order all the time or even have an expectation of actually getting something accomplished. Flexibility is our most important tool, but it can be a teacher's downfall. The combining of these two strengths in a close relationship could be a challenge.

Please note that I am NOT saying that teachers, artists, athletes and so on are bad relationship partners. Of course that's not true. I'm saying that those gifts and talents would probably not blend well with me and my talents, life outlook and thinking patterns.

So, who could you just not be with 24/7, even if they're chock-full of amazing talents and attributes? Be fair to yourself and to a potential future mate/friend. Think of the weak areas in yourself you'd like someone to complement. What areas of strength would you like encouraged and built up? What areas of strength do you possess that could be an encouragement or a complement for someone else? We'll look into the dynamics of relationships more in PART 3, but for now, think about the strengths that would blend well with the kind of person you are.

Likewise, what weak or negative issues can you deal with? What habits or preferences are flat-out intolerable to you? We've already identified some deal-breaking patterns, but what additional issues might you struggle with in a close relationship? Some examples of potential difficult areas are:

- Smoking
- Dog lover or hater
- Neat freak
- Slob/hoarder
- Morning person or Night Person (there's nothing worse than a morning person cheerfully and energetically humming, making coffee, etc. to a night person at 6:00 a.m. My gosh, we've only been asleep four or five hours!)
- Different faith beliefs
- Different political beliefs
- Significant age difference (a BIG issue to consider)
- Vacation preferences
- Excessive ____________ (Fill in this blank. This could be something basically positive like work, exercise, phone calls with Mom, etc., but excessiveness is

usually difficult to compete with for time and attention)

In the smaller issues there's really no right or wrong, or good or bad. Since every human has some flaws and annoying habits and traits, it's just a matter of finding the ones you can live with. Again, be honest with yourself. You're simply listing the traits, habits and character of a good match for you, not determining a person's worth. So, get your pen or pencil and add some items to your list of requirements. Hopefully some things that are either desirable or are unacceptable have come to mind. Build your list as fully and comprehensively as you can!

CHAPTER 15-- FIND SOMEONE WITH GOOD BUMPER STICKERS

Now, this chapter heading isn't necessarily one to be taken literally because many people don't even have stickers on their vehicles (or even have vehicles). The idea is that you need to think about what you want your friend/mate to believe in and how they express it. Take note next time you're on the highway and see what people choose to tell the world about themselves. Many stickers brag about their kids being honor students, or comment on political issues, tout products or services, or any number of things

Sadly, I have noticed an increasing number of vulgar bumper stickers the last few years. One such sticker I saw I cannot even fully put into print and I apologize for the implied vulgarity, but it was "____ you, you ___ing dumb ___." Okay that's just an angry, empty person. Not much doubt about it. I think it's fair to say the driver of that truck is nowhere near being a safe, healthy and happy person who's good relationship material. Yes, I make that judgment based solely on a few words she purchased and stuck to her truck but come ON. She actually spent money on that bumper sticker and invested time to display it on her vehicle where hundreds of hapless people who've probably done no infraction to her whatsoever are forced to see it. It is a very aggressive, angry, even arrogant message designed to put down everyone behind her in traffic. She intends to keep people at a distance. THAT is what she wants people to know about her— she likes dropping the f-bomb, has nothing of value to say to the world, and hates everyone. Maybe she thought it was funny but it seems very sad to me. I prayed for her to lose her baggage of bitterness she apparently carries around because it seems like the load is too much for her and it's spilling over.

What do you want spilling over on a friend or mate's bumper? Now I am speaking literally. Think what a perfect match for you wants to let the world know about him or her. The space on a bumper is limited, so what two or three bits of info would your ideal mate/friend display?

What if you're getting to know someone and you discover to your horror his/her bumper is full of

Republican Party issues stickers and you're a to-the-tips-of-your-toes Democrat? Or there's a sticker that touts the opposite view of an issue that's important to you, such as a "Choose Life" message while your car adornments speak of "Pro Choice?" What if someone's bumper says "Follow Me to Harry's Strip Bar" and you're very opposed to such establishments? Every relationship has agree-to-disagree areas, but what are you willing to be unequally yoked to? Consider what issue might be deal-breakers for you and add those to your list of requirements. Again, be honest---if you feel strongly that Issue 2 (whatever that may be) should not be voted into law, list that as a topic or issue you require a close friend or significant other to agree with you on. Many issues are only mildly important, but some are crucial. It's good to know where you stand and what differing opinions you find unacceptable. Remember, the idea of your Requirements List is that the person matches the list, not that you adjust the list to match the person.

Similarly, what type of vanity plate statements or license plate messages are okay with you? Vanity plates can be whimsical, humorous, inspiring, tongue-in-cheek, or they can advertise their services like "IBUYHOMS" or they can be… well, vain and shallow. How do you feel about "DIVA" or "BSTLVR" or something else that's purely self-praising? If "Diva" got that plate as a whim it might be amusing. If, however, she truly feels like she is a diva, superior and entitled, it might be wise to give serious thought to deepening that relationship. Or not.

While we're on the topic of self-expressing-in-odd-ways, how about message tee shirts, social media posts, and other online messages? It's the same principle. What people choose to outwardly express to the world is often not to be ignored. It's common for prospective employers to look over an applicant's social media posts to be sure that what the applicant is expressing to the world is consistent with the company mission and wants onboard. As a prospective friend or partner, you'd be wise to do the same.

Another thing to consider within this topic of self-expression is how important it is to make sure the person's presentation of self to you is consistent with the messages they put out to the world. For example, if a person assures you, they do not drink but during your Facebook-stalking you find multiple pictures of her or him holding up bottles of beer while wearing a lampshade, there's a disconnect between who they say they are and who they truly are. How many disconnects are you okay with, and over what issues? And, frankly, what level of dumbness are you willing to accept, since gross inconsistencies between their presentation and their posts are so easy to discover?

We've all caught people in untruths. It's said that we are lied to several dozen times every day, and in fact we tell at least one lie a day. It's essential you decide on your standard for untruths in a relationship. Perhaps it's okay if your significant other tells you he or she only ate one piece of cake when it was actually two pieces, (or is it?) but it's probably not okay if they tell you they worked late when in fact you know their office is closed and they couldn't have possibly been where they said they were. While of course you don't want or expect to be lied to, are there times when it's acceptable? What is your standard for honesty, and how do you discern when your standard is broken? After pondering this and reaching a decision that seems reasonable, put it on your list of requirements, maybe in the Absolute Musts column.

Lies in relationships can be deadly. Just ask Sapphira, Ananias' wife whose story is told in Acts 5:1-10. It's a chilling story. In fact, Verse 5 tells us, "great fear came over all who heard of it." In a nutshell, Ananias and Sapphira sold a piece of property, gave some of the money to the apostles but lied and said they gave the full amount. Not giving the full amount wasn't the issue, the lie was what mattered. In fact, Peter says it was a lie to the Holy Spirit (v.3) and to God (v.4). As soon as each of them uttered the lie, they "breathed their last" (verses 5 and 10). Boom, that's it. No more inhaling or exhaling for those two, they're done. Of course, God doesn't deal so resolutely with every lie told (at least not on Earth) but apparently, it's a big deal.

So, we know from God's word truth-telling is a big deal, and we're told by researchers or whoever "they" are that lies are rampant in our daily lives. This means we need to set the standard that we want to live by and commit to NEVER bend on it!

CHAPTER 16-- FIND A PERSON WITH GOOD PATTERNS

"Brethren, join in following my example, and observe those who walk according to the pattern you have in us" Paul writes in Philippians 3:17. So, we're to observe the patterns of others. Hmmm. I believe the meaning here is believers in Christ should follow Paul's example of faithfulness, hope, perseverance, and righteousness received through Christ, and all the other godly traits Paul's example teaches us, but I'm going to take the liberty of focusing on the latter part of the verse that says we're to observe the patterns that are walked.

What life pattern do you want in the people around you? We don't usually get to choose our neighbors, coworkers or family members but we do get to choose who's close to us. These are the people we choose to hang out with, talk over problems with, listen to, and so on. What are the patterns in those people we choose?

I doubt most schools still offer Home Economics, but back in the day at my school (Go Vikings!) girls were required to take at least 1 semester of Home Economics. Oddly, I don't think the curriculum had a thing to do with the actual economics of running a home, which would have been unendingly useful. Instead it dealt with two skills: cooking and sewing. Oh, I wish I had paid more attention in that class because I'd love to be good at those things, but alas I did not so I am not. I do remember, though, we (sort of!) learned how to read the instructions for sewing specific items. These instructions are called patterns, and they're sold in little envelope-like packages. They are, I still think, often extremely difficult to comprehend. Each pattern can make several different clothing items, and the one sewing the item must differentiate which lines go with which item, while also knowing what size guidelines to follow on the pattern, all while trying to lessen the amount of blood lost because of pinning the very thin paper of the pattern to the fabric. It's highly stressful to those of us who are not gifted or coordinated in that area. In fact, as I'm typing I can feel my heart beating faster, and my fingers are hitting the keys of my laptop harder than necessary just remembering the trauma of it all. Give me a second to regroup.

Thanks for staying with me, and yes, I have a good reason for writing about sewing from a pattern. All of us, every day of our lives, are sewing together our lives and we use a pattern of some sort. On Monday we sew a few more stitches into the lives we stitched on Sunday and on Tuesday we add to that, and so on and so on. We sew hundreds of thousands of stitches until we have no more tomorrows, and the entirety of the creation we made is laid out before us. For some people the pattern was chosen for them and they haven't yet changed it to one they like. Other people chose several different patterns and switch from one to another. Still others diligently focus on one chosen pattern. Some people form beautifully seamed creations, while others have missed stitches and bloodstains from the needle pokes. Regardless of how we end up with the pattern and what the end result is, we are all working, one stitch at a time, toward a project that at some point will be our final presentation.

Let's go back to Philippians 3:17 to see what a good pattern looks like. First, we see that in this pattern we're in a family. We're brethren, or siblings. We belong to this group, and we're wanted there. We are not disowned or abandoned. Second, we're offered an invitation to unity. We're invited to join the people who walk according to Paul's example. Third, there's movement. We're following and, presumably, walking toward the same thing Paul is walking toward, which we know from v. 14 is the goal of the prize of being called to heaven by God through Jesus. We are moving toward the ultimate goal of life. Fourth, we get to choose whether we join the walkers or not. We exercise free will in a meaningful, wise way. Finally, we are encouraged to be wise, by observing those already walking in a good pattern. They choose to walk away from destruction and shame (v.19).

What pattern are you using to stitch together your life? Is it like what we read about in Philippians 3:17?

- Are you using a pattern your parents set or one you chose?
- Is this a pattern of love and happy guidance or is it a pattern of destruction

and diminished being, confusion and loneliness?

- Were you given an envelope that contained a pattern of growth and hope but you traded it in for addiction and degradation, or vice-versa?
- Are you following the pattern toward unity and belonging?
- Have you hopped from pattern to pattern, never committing to one, and your completed project is a hodge-podge so far? What will it be a hodge-podge of, and will there be beauty and meaning in it?
- Will your pattern help you reach the prize of being called to heaven?

Returning to the first question in this chapter, what life pattern do you want in the people around you? Knowing that every choice is a stitch in your life project, who you choose to be entwined with takes on enormous importance. Good people will make the project stronger and more gorgeous, while negative people will cause chaos. If you choose "those who walk according to the pattern you have in us" and don't walk with those who are "enemies of the cross of Christ" (v.18), you've chosen wisely and are headed for transformation and His glory (v. 21).

To use another example, in the world of baton-twirling (yes, this world exists, and it's quite exciting!) being "off pattern" during a routine at a competition is a very bad thing. Points are deducted, so the twirler tries her (there are some awesome male twirlers, but the vast majority are female, so I'm going with feminine pronouns here) very best to stay focused and not vary from the pattern of where her feet are pointed and how her baton is positioned. It's one of the first things twirlers learn, and it's such a basic skill that to be off pattern earns immediate pity or disdain from other twirlers and sighs from coaches. Twirlers in general are a warm, kind group of very talented athletes, but still, they disdain an error that's such a basic facet of the sport.

While a twirler is off pattern there are often feelings of anxiety and an urgency to get back on pattern before the routine is ruined. The next toss depends on the pattern of the baton just prior to the toss. Each step determines the success of the next. Advanced twirlers usually handle pattern errors with grace and skill, but I've seen Novice and even Beginner twirlers tearfully lose it and never quite get the routine back on track, therefore scoring badly in the event. I even knew a couple Advanced twirlers who, when they couldn't get back on track, faked falls and limped off the gym floor so they could blame their "ankle injury" for their mistake. The judges weren't fooled, and I doubt anyone else was, either. Maybe I'm just being catty here. My bad. Hee hee. The point is that the pattern is very important and to be off it isn't good.

Obviously, I'm not suggesting you must look for a baton twirler or a seamstress to be your significant other. Although there's a lot to be said for people who can whip together a great dress or keep multiple surprisingly heavy metal sticks spinning in the air in time to music! Let's observe their pattern for our purposes.

Using the baton example, a person who's on pattern is:

- Heading in the right direction—their feet are pointed in the direction that will enable them to go to the next step with no errors

- Moving toward a great prize
- In control of all they're juggling. Their batons are in the right position, either vertical or horizontal, never at a sloppy slant
- Part of a united team
- Using the example of a sewing pattern, a person who's on pattern is:
- Steadily stitching together a project that is strong, beautiful and precious
- Able to join sewing mentors and observe their skills, so they improve their own skills
- Willing to faithfully adhere to the pattern as written, no matter how difficult it may be at times
- Willing to not arrogantly take ownership of the pattern, but joins

other followers of the example that has been set and proven

- Able to trust that a glorious result will be created, even when the pattern maker seems off or doesn't make sense

Take time to ponder these points and others that may occur to you, to decide specifically what a person with a good pattern looks like to you. What is the goal and pace of the movement? Do you want to FIND a person whose goal is the same as yours? Who do you want your brethren and your walkers to be?

CHAPTER 17-- FIND A PERSON WHO FITS A HEALTHY ROLE FOR YOU

Several years ago I went to a day-long women's retreat. You probably know the type—they offer renewal and refreshment and hopefully new friendships and perspectives. I don't remember much about it except the segment about roles. Two very creative ladies who made that presentation had a huge bag full of hats worn by different role-players in life. They had dozens of different hats we figuratively put on for the activities of our daily lives. They pulled out of the bag a chef's hat, a nurse's cap, a fireman's hat, a police officer's cap, a motorcycle helmet, a housekeeper's cap, a beauty queen's tiara, an athlete's helmet, a scientist's goggles, a tennis player's visor (to help see and returning all the balls slamming at us), a Captain's hat, a bus driver's hat, a surgical cap, and on and on and on. It took about ten minutes to empty their bag! They missed nothing! After just a couple minutes I got a little teary because it was becoming clear why I felt so tired and felt overly stretched. We all do so much, and a lot of it's out of our comfort zone and expertise. We often do these things with little conscious thought usually. Something in our path needs doing, so we do it. We perform many roles every day. That's life, and what it requires of all of us.

In a close relationship the roles are much more defined and intrinsic because fewer people are involved and active. Each person in the relationship must perform their adopted role for the relationship to move forward in whatever way it's moving forward. The very relationship is dependent on its members to fulfill their roles with some precision for the relationship to continue its trajectory.

This is where "dysfunction" and "function" begin. For a relationship to be functional, the roles must be clear, even if subconscious, and each member must function within the definition of a certain role toward a common, beneficial goal. An example is any TV cop-show partnership; both members pull toward the common goal of safety and well-being of the citizens in the community. To do this they must each fulfill their roles to each other as assister, supporter, back-up provider, watcher, guard, protector, and the like. If each partner performs their role well, the professional relationship is successful, safe and beneficial to all. If the relationship is dysfunctional, the members aren't pulling toward the same goal and it's not a healthy and beneficial relationship for anyone. The oft-cited example of a dysfunctional relationship is a couple where one is an alcoholic, and the other is an enabler. They're each putting effort into reaching a goal, but it is a goal of devastation, pain and waste. Both the enabler and the alcoholic are performing their respective roles quite well, but it is getting them nowhere good.

So where do these roles originate, what are good ones, and how do they get off-track? To find these answers we must return to the original human relationship—Eve and Adam.

In Genesis 2:20 we read that God saw "there was not found a helper suitable for" or "companion who corresponded to" (NET Bible) Adam, so He created a woman from Adam's rib and brought her to Adam. Adam seemed to have had a sensible and accurate view of Eve, knowing she came from him but not lording that over her. He simply called her a variation of his own name and expressed understanding that she came from his own wonderfully made body. Adam seems quite pleased with this new creation, and the two begin a life of "one-flesh" and unashamed openness. Adam's role was providing the rib for Eve's creation, and Eve's role is to be the helper. "Helper" isn't clearly defined in these verses so we must make a few assumptions that Eve's role included companionship, finishing some of Adam's sentences, coming up with good ideas to add to Adams', helping him carry heavy loads of wood if needed, and so on. Genesis doesn't indicate Eve was created as weaker or stronger, particularly needed protection, inferior or superior. She was simply created from and for Adam.

Since the purpose of creating Eve was to be a helper, we must assume she indeed was a good helper and they were a team. The Holman Christian Standard Bible says that Adam needed a "complement", or that which completes or perfects. Since all that God made was "very good" (v 31), we can assume the two fit together nicely and made the partnership God intended. In fact, this partnership was worth leaving mom and dad for, and clinging entirely to each other (v. 24, paraphrased). That's huge, because "dad" in this case was God the Creator whose love is immense and endless, and all that Adam and Eve knew. I don't think the intention was for Adam and Eve to leave their loving relationship with God, but the man/woman life-mate relationship is pointed out to be above all other human relationships. I believe we can infer that since "they were not ashamed" (v. 25), they never argued or put one another down, never cold-shouldered or were anything but perfectly united.

But then it got ugly. No one seems to be able to fully explain what possessed Eve to listen to the serpent and why on earth Adam went along with the non-God program, but they did, as any human would have. The perfect team was demolished. Their roles were trashed. Adam was no longer the provider of self for Eve and she was no longer a suitable companion. They became hiders, liars, threw each other under bus after bus. Shame and total brokenness ensued and nothing would be the same on earth in this world ever again. Dang. The roles God created were important and perfect. If only humanity could've lived within them.

We have the good, God-made roles still, but added to that are the unhealthy and destructive roles. Double-dang.

Think about your roles in life. Go ahead and list them out. Start with the easier ones, like son or daughter, oldest sibling, your occupation, tasks you do around the house, employer or employee, parenting tasks you do, and continue your list. Put on all the hats you can think of from the bag from the retreat. There are so many of them! If you wrote less than ten or fifteen on your list, you probably need to keep thinking.

Now, go deeper. Get to the real roles you play every day. Are you a rescuer? Are you an avoider? A fighter? Maybe you've become the peacemaker and everyone knows you'll go along with anything in the interest of "peace." Maybe you were the adored baby in your family, and you've carried that role into the present.

ROLES LIST

I've heard the same feedback enough times I have to admit it must be true. I've been told I'm constantly defensive and even "looking for a fight" at times. I don't get out of bed every day swinging and throwing punches at people in my path. In fact, I believe I am quite pleasant and do my best to be kind and soft-spoken. But apparently people sometimes sense an air of defensiveness that comes from the role of defender I adopted as a child. There were endless verbal arrows launched in my household, and I had to either defend against them or be swallowed up by them. Being swallowed didn't appeal to me, so I learned to build an abrasive, chilly, never a patsy, exterior to use when needed. That role served a purpose of survival at the time and has some positives. I very rarely back down from an obstacle on behalf of a client in my career as a social worker and I have excellent boundaries and I'm rarely taken advantage of, and I have righted several wrongs in life. But the role of defender also comes with negatives. That air of defensiveness apparently is not warm and cuddly and inviting. It doesn't match my Goal Statement as it doesn't make me seem like a safe and fun person to be around. I don't draw people to me because I seem prickly and unsafe. Now, truth be told, I often tend to be okay with the thought of repelling people, but it's not how God designed me nor is it the right role for me. We're created for connectedness, so the role of fighter or defender doesn't fit with functional relationships. I'm aware of this aspect of my personality and I make necessary and all possible changes toward health, friendliness, and warmth. I also must be sure to be cautious of close relationships with those who might also live in the role of fighter or a person in the role of victim until I've fully ironed out my defensiveness or a disaster could ensue. The defender role was needed for a while, but it isn't now and progress toward a softer, more open role is necessary.

Think about the role or roles you had to adopt in your childhood. Hopefully it wasn't one of survival, but perhaps it wasn't a great role to continue into your adult relationships, and maybe you don't need that role anymore either. Honestly look at what you're accustomed to so that you can opt to walk toward similar situations or scurry far from that. Let's consider a few fictitious examples:

- "Justin" grew up in a home filled with tension, arguing, slamming doors. His mother was an alcoholic who neglected the kids and family and house. His father, who didn't have a better plan, argued with her constantly, thinking this would help her see she needed to make some changes in herself and her life. Justin went through much of his early life thinking this was normal. He learned to navigate around the hostility by retreating to his room, isolating himself. Most of his emotional needs went unmet. Since this is his version of normal, Justin usually leans into out of control women. He assumes the role of overwhelmed rescuer. Since he never developed healthy emotional expressions, he reverts to what worked for him as a child and withdraws from those around him.

- "Brian" grew up with divorced parents. He was shifted from his mom to his dad and back again. Neither particularly wanted to be a parent, and he was left largely on his own. Brian has no mature skills to bring into adulthood. He now lives in his father's basement, drinking and playing video games. He is an avoider of life and relationships. He occasionally rises up from the basement to find a rescuer. Since rescuers often have to be fairly functional, capable adults to be in the role of rescuer, his relationships burn out quickly once the rescuer decides she doesn't want to be drained anymore.
- "Samantha" was an only child, adored by her parents. Their lives

revolved around her, always. She can't figure out why the men she dates don't live their lives completely to her specifications. She finally finds one she can mold and teach to idolize her as she should be idolized. She has adopted the role of princess, and her relationships will have difficulty when her "throne" is shaken.

- "Hailey" grew up in a single parent family but was wonderfully loved, protected, and encouraged by her mother. She excelled in school and sports and became a talented caring doctor. She's overwhelmed by the father-sized hole in her heart and seeks to fill the void by endless and constant boyfriends and dates. She usually has a bevy of boyfriends-in-waiting lined up, just in case. She knows deep down that the boyfriends can never fill the empty spot, and drinks often to not feel her pain. She has adopted the role of pursuer. She will pursue that which she can never find but may keep pursuing.

These examples are all too real. In fact, most of us can probably relate to at least some aspects of them. The questions to ask and answer for yourself is, "What unhealthiness am I used to?", and "How am I searching for a person to restore that sense of normalcy, whether or not it's healthy? The book How We Love by Milan & Kay Yerkovich provides an excellent look at roles or styles, as the Yerkovichs name them, that we take on in relationships. If you are struggling to identify your past and current roles, the book may be a helpful resource for you. AFTER you finish this book, of course.

There are many questions to ponder in determining a good match for you to have a good relationship with healthy roles. Some examples include:

- What is normal to you?

- How were you seen in your family of origin?
- Did you have multiple families?
- What was your role; what were you expected to do in your family?
- What were you taught to expect from others?
- What were you taught to expect from yourself?
- You were taught how to relate to others, but how....as a care-taker, butt-of-all-jokes, protector, achiever, or something else?
- Who do you usually gravitate toward? Do you tend to lean into people who need you? Or people who don't need you, and in fact ignore you?
- Do you usually go toward or away from demanding, controlling people, or people who don't require deep emotional intimacy?

- How does your role in current relationships match up with your Goal Statement? If it matches well, great! If not, you have some work to do, either on the role you've adopted in life, or in your Goal Statement. It's not possible to want to be a certain type of person and to behave as another type, and still feel satisfied and healthy in who you are as a person. For example, let's say your Goal Statement includes being an assertive person who's a good friend to others but who also requires friends to be respectful and reciprocal of you. That's a good goal. However, if you frequently accept middle-of-the-night calls from sobbing and/or drunk "friends" who won't even thank you the next day for your listening ear let alone dream of answering a call for help from you, then how you live is not in sync with your Goal Statement.

Take a moment and think about your developing years. What was expected of you, and how were love and even punishment handed out? Did you need to be dependent or independent to survive in your family? What messages did you hear? Maybe talking to your siblings or other family members might help bring some things to mind. You might already know this very well, or perhaps you need to give it deep pondering and even jot down notes.

The role you played in your family of origin probably carried into your work as an adult. For instance, "Samantha" from our example became a teacher because she wanted to be sure 20 or 25 little faces looked at her all day and did her bidding because this felt normal to her. Of course, not all teachers are Samanthas, using children to get their own needs met, but in her case, it was a comfortable, practical way to continue what felt normal to her. It worked pretty well. She was a good teacher who was effective at teaching kids new and needed skills, she was loved by students and parents, and she earned a fair (although lower than what she is worth!) wage. But perhaps if she had really thought about why teaching seemed like a good fit she might've opted for a different life career. Maybe teaching in order to continue what she knew to be normal wasn't the best option after all.

Now that you've duly pondered these questions and have reached some insight, focus on the next questions you need to ask:

- How are you currently dealing with the normalcy to which you became accustomed?
- Do the people you generally hang out with remind you of anyone? Is that a good thing or a bad thing?
- Do you see any redundancy in the roles you play at work or with friends, etc?
- Are you in the same roles now as you were in your childhood, and, if so, is that healthy and enjoyable?

These issues and questions might seem like they belong in PART 1 where we explored BEING the Right

Person but after some wiggling and adjusting, I opted to put them in PART II because your answers to these questions are important to FINDING the right person for a close relationship. You might have the best, most perfect roles in your life and you may be the healthiest person in the room, but if you don't choose a role that will, like Eve was supposed to, complement a relationship partner, the relationship won't be what God wants for you.

FIND someone whose roles healthily complement your own. Take some time now to consider what you've discovered about your tendencies toward certain roles in comparison to what a healthy complement to those roles looks like. For instance, if you know you tend to take on a care-taker role, you must decide if you want to continue that in a relationship with a constantly needy person. I'm not saying you should or shouldn't want a constantly needy person; I'm encouraging you to be aware of the roles both you and the other person would play. Look at the costs and rewards therein and determine if that's what you want. Remember, the goal of a perfect, unified relationship is to complement each other. That goal was battered in the Garden of Eden, but it's still the original goal Genesis describes in the only example of a perfect human relationship.

CHAPTER 18-- FIND A PERSON YOU WANT TO CO-PARENT WITH— OR NOT

This one is a life-changer. Don't overlook it.

Co-parenting successfully includes and requires equal yoking but it goes much further than that and deserves its own deep consideration. You may FIND someone with whom you can yoke equally in terms of faith, priorities, and so on. That is great and wonderful (More on this issue in Part III, Chapter 20.) but it's not enough. There are unique issues to consider if you plan on bringing children into your relationship—or if you don't.

That's the first question, isn't it? "Do I or do I not want children? Do I want the joys, the pain, the inconvenience, the laughter, love, financial cost, pride, endless work and sacrifice, turmoil, risk, growth, fulfillment, and so on that having a child requires and provides?" This is a crucial question to answer before a child appears in the cabbage patch. Once you're sure of your answer to this question, your path should be set; FINDing a person who shares this answer. There's no compromise on the issue of whether or not to have children; one person of a couple cannot talk the other into wanting or not wanting children. Children do tend to be full time, so there's no "well, I dunno-- let's do it for a year or two and see how it goes." It's either all in or all out. Opinions and desires can change over time, but it is vitally important to FIND a person who is like-minded at the on-set.

So, assuming the answer is "Nope, no thank you" on the issue of reproduction, what then is your life plan? Do you want to travel, be a missionary, live the dream in the suburbs, build a business empire, live on a commune in the forest, or...? The right person for you is someone on the same page, or at least in the same book, right?

If you do want children, then you're on a path to FIND the right parenting partner. Yikes. This one is very tough, because how do you know how someone parents until... well, until they do? Here are some clues to ponder:

- How much interaction with children is healthy? Do you want to parent with someone who's never been within ten feet of a child, or do you want someone whose

17 nieces and nephews adore them, and they spend dozens of hours a week with them? Where is a healthy boundary, and how can you see it clearly?

- What family background do you want your parenting partner to come from?
- How involved do you want your children's mom/dad to be in their lives? What traits and patterns should you look for that may indicate a good match?
- What are your weaknesses and strengths that'll impact your parenting skills? What do you need in a partner to complement them?
- What kind of extended family do you want involved with your children? How will you draw a boundary if the extended family is unhealthy?

Sadly, the divorce rate is very high. It shouldn't be. Mature, healthy adults should be sharp enough to marry and reproduce only with other mature, healthy adults so all should be rosy, but that's just not how it is in our world. More people obviously need to read this book! Or, much better, read and put into practice Biblical concepts including love, patience, long-suffering, selflessness, and all the other wonderful qualities God has given us the power to choose to pursue. Since the divorce rate is extremely high, unfortunately, it's wise and practical to consider a worst-case scenario. You must FIND someone you're absolutely positive, after honestly looking at all angles, will be a person you are comfortable dropping your kids off with for the weekend. Think this through for a few moments. Hopefully you and your kids will never have to go through the pain of a divorce, but if the unthinkable happens, you'll most likely have to leave the kids you adore with the person that you couldn't work things out with. Staggeringly horrifying, isn't it? That's why it's so important to BE the healthiest person you possibly can be and FIND the healthiest, best match that you possibly can find. It isn't just fun-n-games or a whim---partnering up with someone and creating a human being is serious stuff. Serious.

PART II CONCLUSION

Woo-hoo! You've finished reading two-thirds of the book! Do you feel more confident of yourself because now you have a map to get where you want to go? Do you have a clearer picture of who you need to FIND for a close relationship? Oh, I hope so! Let's finish strong with Part III because it's important to think things through once you've BEcome the right person and FOUND a great person for you!

As with Part I, I encourage you to jot down anything you think was missed in Part II. Simply because I didn't mention it on these pages doesn't mean it's not a valid point. Your thought is probably a great one I missed, so add it and ponder it as you move forward.

NOTES ON PART II

PART III-- HAVE THE RIGHT RELATIONSHIP

What, exactly, is a right relationship? It isn't simply being "in love" because that's emotion-based, changeable and unreliable. We cannot base our definition of a Right Relationship on who we happen to feel in love with at a particular time, but how do you figure out what the right one looks like? Since we only have one example of a perfectly right relationship, we must look at Eve and Adam again. The absolute, perfect rightness of their relationship was brief, only a few verses, but let's see if we can glean any helpful insights.

First, we see, presumably, amazement and delight from Adam when he sees Eve and we can imagine his awed tone as he speaks of her. Can't you just see him jumping up and down with joy saying "WOW! This one You've made isn't furry and stinky like the other creatures! She kinda looks like me, with the legs and arms and two eyes and ears and......whoa! There are some awesome differences, too! I'm not alone anymore! I can't wait to talk with her and listen to her and share life with this one!" Adam definitely sees the difference with Eve's creation as opposed to all the other creatures God made. He sees that this one is actually part of him! She is from his very body and it sounds to me like he is lovingly and protectively possessive of her... "she was taken out of ME." He knows she is special and to be treasured.

Secondly, their connection was absolute—they were "one flesh." I have often heard this phrase as a reference to intercourse when two bodies are in fact joined and can be considered one, but I believe "one flesh" is meant to go far deeper than that. I can almost see the Lord slapping His forehead when He hears us make that connection, because humans are so short-sighted and we miss His depth of blessing so often. I believe "one flesh" means if a wife has a headache, the husband ought to be getting the acetaminophen before she even asks, and the wife should know her husband is feeling frustrated before he even tells her what the jerk at work did! If the husband stubs his toe, the wife's first response should be "OW", as if it's her own toe throbbing. Further, the wife must know she can trust her man to get her some painkillers, and the husband must know that his wife will see his angst and he can trust her to understand and provide comfort. Just as a man and woman understand and care for their own physical being, mental functioning, and emotional state, being one flesh demands they give equal consideration and care to each other.

"One flesh" tells us only together can they become a whole. If Adam plus Eve equals one, then Adam cannot be a whole one, nor can Eve, because one plus one equals two, not one. In an ideal relationship, one person's deficits are covered by the other, and one person's strengths are lent to the other's weaknesses. We don't know specifically what Eve's deficits were or what qualities Adam used to compensate for them, and vice-versa, but we know that the oneness was perfect and complete. Together, they were able to "git 'er done" and accomplish anything, perfectly complementing each other while doing so.

Thirdly, they felt no shame (v. 25). The full verse explains they were both naked and weren't ashamed. At first glance this seems to say that they weren't ashamed of their nakedness, but on deeper consideration we can see the verse doesn't limit the reason for their lack of shame. I only found one version of the Bible that linked the nakedness and lack of shame, as opposed to a couple dozen other versions that didn't, so I think it is safe to say, "They were not ashamed", period.

Shame-free in a relationship....can you imagine? Isn't shame a base issue in most of our difficulty having the perfect, emotionally intimate relationship full of trust and safety? It must be a huge issue because it's the first consequence of the first couple's sin. The immediate result of eating the fruit was they got busy sewing to cover what they now know as differentness, or not-oneness. They were, like we so often are, ashamed of being different from one another--and possibly not acceptable. We hide ourselves and lie to avoid rejection, which then builds up the layers of imperfection. We avoid eye contact because we want to hide our emotions or we avoid having the honest conversation we know we need to have because we feel exposed, fearful and ashamed of who we are. Shame is pervasive and insidious and it was never meant to be a part of a relationship. The relationship our Creator meant for us to have is one without the barrier of shame. Eve and Adam had that but lost it.

The final insight seen in the brief perfection of Adam and Eve's relationship is they were stronger together. The serpent approached only one of them, not both. Verse 6 of Genesis 3 tells us Adam was on-site; he was "with her" but still the serpent dealt only with Eve. The serpent was crafty, so we can assume he manipulated this situation in the most effective way possible. That meant dealing with only one of the couple. Together they were impenetrable. Together they were as one, and no manipulation could get past them, because if one weakened the other rose to the occasion and lent their strength to the situation.

We see from that one brief picture of a perfect relationship it must have whole-hearted and joyful appreciation of the other, a deep and unwavering connection with no room for shame or anything less than acceptance and grace. They shared unity free of chips or fissures. That's the essence of the relationship God intended for us, but HOW do we even come close to that?

Many people would think completing or even minimally pondering Parts I and II is all it takes to go forth and enjoy the perfect relationship. Let's assume you're now a perfect package of health, awareness, and all the things we've been discussing, and you know exactly who you are hoping to find. Can you now assume that Being and Finding equals the Right Relationship? Sadly, no. Even if you find someone who meets every item on your Requirements List, a relationship could still be 'off' with that person. Logically, it shouldn't be, right? It should be a matter of course that if you're healthy and strong and you find someone equally healthy with strong traits you admire and need, it should be a match made in, well, Heaven. But it's just not that way with human beings. A really great person could be a crummy match for another really great person. Sigh.

So how do you do the best you can to ensure that your most significant relationships—romantic as well as close friends—are the strongest that they can be? You've done the hard work of Parts I and II, but how do you take your new awareness and strength and build it into something that you are meant to HAVE?

CHAPTER 19-- HAVE CLEAR VISION— LOSE THE BLINDERS

Horses often wear what are called "blinders." They're firm leather attachments that prevent them from seeing to the sides or behind them. Blinders are put on a horse so it's unable to be distracted or fearful of what may be happening around it as it moves forward. Blinders are great for horses, (I'm guessing here, I really don't know. Seems like they must serve a good purpose) but they're HORRID for people. People SHOULD be aware of everything going on. Being oblivious to what is going around you invites danger. Don't invite danger.

We have probably all seen hilarious videos of people so distracted by their phones—blinders, if you will-- they fail to realize they are about to walk into a pole or closed door, etc. The funniest such video I've seen is one where a young woman is so busy texting she walks into a fountain and falls head-over-heels into the water. Possibly staged, but I still laughed nonetheless. She wasn't paying attention to what was happening around her, so she ended her outing wet, embarrassed, probably with a ruined phone, and as a social media joke. I'm sure she probably lived through it just fine, but her day would've been much better if she'd been aware and focused on her surroundings and where she was heading.

God specifically made for Adam someone who was "suitable" for him because He didn't want him to be alone. Alone isn't good. He'd already created countless creatures, "but for Adam there was not found a helper suitable for him" (Gen 2:20). Even though there were countless creatures, it didn't mean they were suitable for Adam. An octopus is a profoundly awesome creature but it wouldn't work well in a close relationship with a human being. The human would drown in the ocean and the octopus would die on land. They aren't suitable for one another. Both wonderful creations, but a terrible match.

Similarly, just because you find a wonderful person, it doesn't mean he or she is necessarily suitable for you. You might have the right person, but the wrong relationship. This is where the blinders MUST come off! The question becomes can the relationship can be honed, or is it just plain wrong for you and needs to end.

There are almost endless differences in every relationship. Differences make us grow, learn and form a stronger bond. A difference doesn't necessarily mean unsuitable. When a "difference" becomes an "issue" there may be problems.

We all probably know at least one couple who are both great people individually but together are a disaster. We stand at the sidelines and watch as they struggle and sometimes even, sadly, crash and burn. This is probably because, despite doing the work to BE the healthy, thriving people they were created to be and to FIND someone of similar health and productivity they didn't look closely at the relationship. They didn't do the work which meant they could in fact be "suitable" (Gen. 2:18). He liked her and she liked him and they went happily toward the aisle assuming their mutual wonderfulness and being in love would carry them through. Sometime after eating the wedding cake however, trouble hit and their assumption dimmed. The blinders came off and they saw the awful truth laid out The relationship seemed discordant and even hopeless at times. There may even have been some absolute deal-breakers foolishly avoided or ignored.

In full disclosure I admit that my current marriage was built just like that. I worked hard to BE a healthy person and I FOUND a wonderful man with almost all the qualities on my Requirements List, but we failed to do the work to carefully examine our relationship, and difficulties have abounded. We are both basically super people with lots of good qualities, but it takes an enormous amount of work for us to communicate effectively and enjoy one another. It sometimes feels like we're as far as we can be from being "one". I have no doubt God brought us together (sometimes I wonder WHAT He was thinking!) and that we're where we're supposed to be. But I also have no doubt that, if we had done the work on our actual relationship, we would be there a lot happier and more productive! We didn't look at crucial differences in our personalities, our styles and quirks, and so on, and so we failed to explore and resolve or at least accept these differences prior to starting a lifelong commitment. We had blinders on because it was easier and less disruptive.

That was a huge and costly mistake. It's taken a lot of years to get to a place of reasonable comfort, trust and joy in our relationship because we failed to see what we needed to see.

So, what are your blinders hiding? What traits, habits, beliefs, preferences which you find unacceptable are you not looking at in your relationship? All relationships have issues. If you don't take off the blinders and bravely and honestly look at the issues you have—all relationships have issues!—you'll likely find yourself wishing you had.

Do you feel a "list time" coming up? Oh, you know me so well by now! Yes, it's list time, but this time there will be multiple lists. Assuming you're in a relationship that seems promising as a potential "forever" relationship, particularly marriage, it's a smart idea to work together and individually to make a list of possible land mines in your relationship. Each person should make a list of the issues they see. Then compare the two lists and agree on a final, single one.

This is NOT a time to complain about the other person! This is time to commit to looking at the issues, big as well as small, that could eventually "tear asunder". For instance, had I been wise enough to make this list, I should not have listed "he has the sense of humor of a pole" because the actual issue is that "we have different senses of humor and do not laugh at the same things." That's a pretty big issue I wish I had genuinely looked at without blinders, because we miss a lot of joy when we often don't laugh at the same things. It isn't that one of us has a superior sense of humor, the issue is that we differ in what amuses us and the importance we place on laughter. If we had made an Issues List, we might've been able to avoid a lot of disappointment and frustration by at least considering this as an issue, calling it such, and committing to either dealing with it or letting it be the deal-breaker of moving forward.

Potentially problem-causing issues within a relationship might be:

- Negative feelings during communication. We've all heard over and over that communication is the key to any relationship and that is true. But just as important is the undercurrent of emotion during a conversation. Are the emotions for both parties generally positive and upbeat, confident and trusting what's said will be received safely and respectfully? Is either person frequently fearful of the response they'll get when they voice a preference, concern or idea?

- Recreational preferences
- Family-of-origin involvement or over-involvement
- Untreated history of abuse
- Untreated addiction, and/or probability of relapse
- Deeply held political beliefs---in some political climates this can be a dangerous item on which to differ
- Deeply held moral beliefs
- History of deceptiveness
- History of cheating
- Parental styles and philosophies, including history of being parented as well as current or anticipated style of parenting children

- Both individual roles, as we talked about in Part II. What are the roles, and do they healthfully blend?
- A feeling of a lack of mutual respect
- Differing priorities
- Unproductive conflict management—yelling, avoiding, bullying, etc.

Once you've completed your own list and compared it with your significant person's list it's time to clearly see, express and discuss the issues on your list. Try to agree on a few top issues as the main list to work through. Boldly and honestly bring up any issues that might be hidden or glossed over. Don't hide or gloss. That serves no purpose in a healthy relationship. And go deep. Talk about WHY these items are issues. What feelings of fear, hurt, abandonment or shame does the specific issue bring forth? Trust in the safe handling of feelings is the root of any strong, lasting relationship.

This may take hours, days or weeks of one-on-one discussion or even months in a counselor's office. Good! Get help with the issues if they're bigger than you can handle on your own! The important thing is bringing the issues into the light. No covering up, no denying, no blinders; these things invite pain and loneliness. Burn your blinders because they have no place in a healthy adult's life. Rejoice in the strengths of your relationship but acknowledge the weak areas and look at them in full light.

ISSUES LIST

What if the issues are massive and irresolvable? Most things, if seen and dealt with honestly, can be resolved, negotiated, or at least accepted, but some issues cannot. Some things are simply bigger than what can fit into this specific relationship. It's ok to walk away. It's preferable to walk away from a relationship that just isn't "suitable" for you. For example, if your roles cannot blend well and it would most likely result in frustration and discord, or one person is greatly and unresolvedly uncomfortable with the other's family, and so forth, it's ok to discontinue the relationship. If something is un-fixable in a relationship and it's harmful or is likely to bring heartache and dissolution, do everyone a favor and walk away.

"OMG, NO!!!" you might be thinking. "No, no, NO. I MUST keep this relationship because it's all I have and no one better will come along. I can just look the other way when he/she _______________ (insert specific issue here) ten times a day. I'm not worth any more than this. It's not that big a deal." That's dumb thinking. Just plain dumb. For heaven's sake, if you're really thinking these kinds of thoughts, you're not ready to move forward in this or any relationship! Go back to Part I and work harder with it! Take a breath, lift your head, stand up taller, act like the adult you are, and do the wise and right thing! You'll find another relationship, and the next one will be stronger because YOU are stronger! You do NOT have to stay in a weak relationship, and you do NOT have to live with blinders on! You're not doing yourself, the other person, or anyone who cares about you a favor volunteering for pain and danger by not facing up to the critical issues that need attention!

CHAPTER 20-- HAVE A RELATIONSHIP WITH EQUAL YOKING

Another farm animal reference. Really? Hey, roots are roots—the girl can leave the countryside, but the countryside never leaves the girl. Yep, "yoke" is a farming concept. It's the do-hickey wooden thing two animals are harnessed with so they pull together to complete a task like plowing a field. There's no way, when yoked, the draft animals can go different directions. If yoked, two animals will plow the same field in the same direction, with no confusion, contemplation, or hesitation.

Most of us who have been in Christian circles long enough have heard this analogy several times. A Christian couple must be heading in the same direction, plowing the same field so to speak. It is a word picture of unity. 2 Corinthians 6:14 tells us (my paraphrase) not to be unequally yoked with unbelievers because going one way doesn't blend with going the opposite way. Specifically, this passage refers to those who follow Jesus should walk in righteousness, not lawlessness and in light, not darkness. Pretty straightforward, right? Makes a lot of sense, as Scripture usually does. An example is if I'm working hard to become a police officer I shouldn't be closely entwined with someone who cherishes breaking the law, as it is not a good match and will not provide unity. Those two lifestyles cannot blend because they're opposites. There may be some similarities between both parties. Maybe they enjoy the same kind of movies, laugh at the same type of jokes, have the same friends, and so on but the core issue is the opposites of a love of lawlessness versus a love of righteousness. These aren't unifying. As the police officer, I cannot comfortably attend a banquet honoring my beloved as winner of the Best Overall Crook of the Year. Likewise, my lawless beloved cannot comfortably attend the Policeman's Ball. In this example, I'm plowing a completely different field from my beloved.

What is the yoking of your relationship and its participants? What "field" are you plowing, and what's the desired outcome? Similarly, what "field" and outcome does the other person in the relationship have? Can you picture the two of you as happy little oxen, harnessed together going in the same direction toward the same goal, in the same field producing the same crop?

The concept of unequal yoking seems most poignant in issues of faith. On any given Sunday in church pews everywhere women and men are sitting alone because their spouse doesn't go to church. How sad. I've known many women who are part of this lonesome scene, and they're... lonesome. Actually, for a few years long ago, I was one of these women and it was in fact very lonely and sad, and.... empty. My young children and I would come home from an hour or two in church and be alone in our experience; we couldn't share with husband/daddy what we experienced or thought because we knew he didn't care much and couldn't relate. What we held so dear and important fell flat in a conversation attempt and there was a huge void.

How can a relationship be healthy, strong and growing if the two people in it differ on such a huge issue as God and our relationship with Him? No matter what faith is followed, how can one person move toward that faith and receive all the benefits of that movement while in the background the other is left standing with his/her mouth open, looking around? If a Jewish person who loves the richness, traditions and teachings of Judaism begins a relationship with an atheist, can there be unity? Can their two hearts ever really meet? The person of faith understands there's Someone who is a Creator, and they're humbled before that Creator, but the atheist believes, I presume, there's no superior Being, but we humans "got this" and are the makers and controllers of our universe and selves. What a different outlook! Complete opposites! How can we think such humility and such arrogance can intertwine? One will overcome the other.

In both newscasts and church videos I've seen pollsters ask random people what do they believe happens after death. Some people answer with the Gospel, some answer with "That's it, we turn to dust" responses, and some say they don't know. A few--to my amazement, horror and complete disdain—respond they simply don't care. Geez, people, shouldn't you at least CARE? Seems to me we oughta at least take responsibility to have an opinion and live accordingly since we need to get this one right, above all other life questions! There're no do-overs on this one, so we'd better do our best to land on the correct side or we might find out we should've cared after all! That rant over, two people in a close relationship must have similar answers to this question or there is deep discord. "I don't know" might squeak through combined with another answer, but a relationship will be weak without sharing a fundamental base. Other combinations will have an even weaker base. Opposites don't form a good, well-yoked base.

The approach to faith in something greater is a much more important issue than "what do I do on Sunday mornings?" (or Passover, or Ramadan, or whatever the expression of faith may be) although that's a valid question worth exploring. The issue of faith or religion determines our path, how we view ourselves and our importance, the basis for our morality, how we treat people and what's vitally important to us. It's huge, yet often couples who've found the "right person" in other ways skip over this issue. Fatal error. Again, don't volunteer for trouble and discord. Make sure you HAVE a relationship that's yoked together on the same faith path. Eventually holidays will roll around and there will be hurt feelings at one person's disinterest, or there will be disagreements or apathy about raising the children in a particular faith. Sitting alone on Sunday mornings will get old. Why risk putting yourself—and your loved one—through this heartache?

There are other paths that require strong yokes. Topics like how many—if any—children you will have, where you will live, navigating family involvement, socialization, careers, ministry, and on and on are all issues that deserve a check to make sure your relationship is traveling with a well-moving yoke. Decide what issues in life are important, ascertain the goals and evaluate your movement toward the goals. Picture your movement toward your goals. Are your oxen faces content or are they twisted in frustration or turned away from each other, pulling to go in opposite directions? Once again like with all the possible issues in your relationship, take off the blinders! Be brave enough to see and discuss differences now rather than later! It's so much easier to acknowledge differences and plan around them in some way than be blind-sided or, even worse, stuck! This is an excellent conversation to have with a counselor if necessary to iron out problem areas or, if need be, to let go of a relationship that just isn't suitable.

Let's take a closer look at deeply held priorities in addition to faith because it is immensely helpful to consider your priorities as individuals and as a couple. What are the goals of your relationship in the areas of:

- Parenting
- Roles/Power
- Building One Another Up
- Finances/Wealth
- Education/Career
- Retirement
- Family/Friends Interactions
- All of the other issues you might hold in high importance.

There are almost endless important areas in a relationship, and certainly no two people can match 100%, all the time forever. Situations change, people change and sometimes perspectives change. Entering and building a long-term relationship requires great trust, faith and quite a lot of flexibility in some areas, but rock-solid adherence to other areas is a must. The question is: which areas demand steadfastness, and which can shift?

Hopefully by now you've learned or confirmed what's important to you, and you've built confidence in those ideals and know they're valuable and belong in a close relationship. You've moved beyond letting another person influence you to downplay those things you hold most dear... right?

This is an excellent time to remind you of Chapter 19—Lose the Blinders! An honest look at the trajectory of a relationship and your future together might be difficult but oh-so-necessary. It's possible two great people with two great priority sets are not, in fact, able to HAVE the right relationship. For example, although one person's priority to live in Uganda for ten years as a missionary is a great one, it probably doesn't blend well with the other person's priority of living forever in a small Midwestern town in the U.S. caring for his/her ailing mother, which is also a fine priority. This needs to be honestly evaluated. There really isn't room for compromise in this instance. This is not the time to blindly say, "Well, yeah, we want completely different things, but we love each other and it'll all work out somehow." Maybe it can work out, but probably not without a lot of honest examination of priorities, life goals and probably making some painful adjustments. Or maybe it won't work out: this could be an unsuitable pairing, and a resolution must be made. Remember, the goal is to HAVE the most-right relationship possible. A sharp contrast in important priorities doesn't lend itself to that goal.

CHAPTER 21-- HAVE A RELATIONSHIP WITH SEXUAL INTEGRITY

This one is, obviously, for relationships of a man/woman romantic nature. Those of you who are reading this book to boost your friendship skills can go grab a quick latte. Muffin, too, while you're at it.

NO THIS SHIP HAS NOT SAILED! NO this isn't old-school, outdated, fuddy-duddy stuff. Yes, I do know what year it is. Respecting sex in a marriage is SO MUCH of how a lasting, honored, and honorable relationship grows. Hopefully, you pondered the content of Part 1, Chapter 10 and you have a deeper understanding of the specialness of a sexual relationship. It isn't to be trifled with, tossed aside or used excessively. The specialness of sex is timeless.

The state of nakedness and the act of joining his parts to her parts is something to hold and protect in highest honor. Think of it---this part is just hanging there with no place to go, while this part has nothing to attach to. It's a picture of incompleteness. All other movable, outer parts have a reason for existing on their own; arms reach, legs walk, fingers clutch, toes balance. The penis just... dangles. Oh, it pushes out urine but surely that could've been handled with a number of design options. Likewise, all other orifices have a reason to exist on their own; ears hear, the mouth eats and speaks (hopefully not simultaneously!) the anus— eww!, and the nostrils breathe and let in smells for the olfactory system. The vagina just ... waits. The dangling penis was made for the waiting vagina, and vice-versa. Seems like a great design, and it is. Uncovering, exploring, and utilizing those parts with another person is meant to be a joining, unifying thing of joy.

So why doesn't this joy-producing, oneness-building gift of creation cement marriages together? Why is the divorce rate so high? Certainly, many factors feed into a divorce, but a huge contributor is we as humans no longer view sex as a perk of only marriage. We take the liberty of "perking" ourselves silly! Current data shows the average number of sex partners is 11 to 13 for young adults over their lifetimes. Since it's impossible to be one with 13 people, the ideal picture has been decimated and marriage has lost much of its specialness. However, marriage is still the ideal held by our society. If you don't believe that, look at the bridal/wedding industry! In the US alone, it is estimated to be worth close to $55 Billion. That's a "b," not even an "m." This is huge. Or, notice how many women refer to their boyfriends as "fiancés" even when they are not sporting a ring or have a date set and the "fiancé" in question refers to the girlfriend in lesser terms like girlfriend or—horrors!—"baby mama." Really. Pay attention to this in casual conversation, or on talk shows. It's comical but at the same time so sad. Americans want the dream—marriage, picket fence, the pretty picture-- but too few couples take the time and self-control to build up the foundation of their marital relationship by protecting the sacredness of their sexual relationship.

YOU can do better! You can choose to protect the boundaries of marriage by not allowing it to be tainted by sexual experience with anyone but your spouse and you within the unique relationship of marriage. Set a standard of no-tolerance for outside interference! But HOW?

First, don't have sexual relations prior to marriage. Pretty obvious, really. It's also extremely difficult to accomplish, especially in our culture that expects and even celebrates sex quickly in a relationship. But, if that standard is set from the get-go, you have a far better chance of a lifetime of mutual sexual purity and satisfaction. If you welcome sex into a not-married situation, you've then invited sexual impurity. If a woman, for instance, welcomes sex in a relationship before the vows are said and cake is eaten, she's basically communicating to her husband she doesn't value monogamous, pure sex in their relationship. The dye has been cast. The door is open to a lot of things a married couple doesn't want. The groundwork's laid and the foundation set. The message of "Eh, let's skip the usual rules of marriage and make our own" can be a fatal, painful message later in the relationship.

Second, allow no other sexual input into your relationship. Don't tolerate or excuse cheating, porn, 900-line phone calls, flirtatiousness, or anything that invites anyone other than you and your spouse into the sexual relationship. The Bible tells us in Hebrews 13:4 the marriage bed should be kept pure and undefiled. Since our Creator created marriage to include two people only, that's how many people should be in the marriage bed. Only two. Sex is meant to build intimacy and specialness. Closeness and cherishing cannot occur with multiple partners in the way a marriage is meant to build.

When I worked on a crisis hotline we occasionally, sadly, got "perp" calls. These creeps would, unbeknownst to us, use our voices for their sexual pleasure even though what we were saying was never of a sexual nature EVER. Yeah, ICK. We'd treat the call as a legitimate request for help until it became obvious it wasn't. I always told my husband about these calls when they happened because, technically, I was part of some nameless guy's sexual activity that afternoon. (So, so ICK!!) Of course, I wasn't even a tiny bit of a willing participant in this activity but, still...I felt it worth mentioning to Hubs, in the interest of full disclosure and openness. I didn't allow even this pathetic sexual input to lurk in our marriage. His comments were minimal when I'd tell him, but I was building on the "no tolerance' standard we'd built.

This is a fairly extreme example, but it illustrates there should be no secrets or untold activities in this area, harmless as they may seem. A business lunch with an opposite-sex rep---needs to be shared. An hour spent on the computer looking at porn—needs to be told and dealt with. Someone at work coming on to you---yep, tell it. Don't hide it. Don't invite a third person into the purity you're building. Temptations and dangers can grow out of almost nothing, so be vigilant! Be vigilant about both your behavior and your beloved's behavior. Is he or she as transparent as they can be, giving you access to their emails, phone history, etc. Set a firm, agreed-to standard for integrity in this area before the pastor announces "Mr. and Mrs." Anything less than 100 percent integrity will not go well. Sooner or later it will come back to hurt you.

CHAPTER 22-- HAVE A RELATIONSHIP THAT HAS NOT INCLUDED COHABITATION

This, THIS is the reason I wanted so badly to write this entire book. I DETEST cohabitation/living together/shacking up or, as I prefer to call it "living as an unpaid whore, maid, and cook" (somewhat paraphrasing Dr. Laura Schlessinger). It's the STUPIDEST arrangement humans have ever thought of! Even without my Christian faith that teaches me that I'm worth so much more than that to my Creator, I would detest shacking up. It is a stuuupid arrangement because:

- When living with a boyfriend/girlfriend, you have no legal protection whatsoever in most states. In many states you have no legal rights to protect yourself if/when the relationship crumbles. If you've brought someone into your home, you often have no legal way to evict the bum when you're ready to do so. You have no piece of paper that protects you. I can imagine some snickers right now---- "Yeah, it's just a stupid piece of paper" you say. Well, then, if paper is so unimportant, give me the title to your car. You can send it via my email right now. Yeah. Paper matters.

- If you live with a boy/girlfriend, you're telling the world that they're not necessarily a 'keeper', that you don't feel they're worthy of a life-long commitment. You expect someone better might come along, and you want an easy out. Don't deny this: if the message were different the level of commitment would be different.
- If you live with a girl/boyfriend you're allowing them to say the above about YOU! That's really the kicker here---WHY would ANYone be okay with that??? Over my

dead, rotting and speechless body would I ever allow that message to be given about me! Even in my sickest, neediest, most insecure days I never would have found that to be acceptable. That's saying a lot, because I was super-needy and pitiful, but I wasn't totally devoid of self-respect to this degree. Well, I might've been, but I certainly wasn't going to broadcast it!

- THINK about this message that cohabitating gives! Is it really okay with you? Do you really want to go to your friends' house this weekend knowing that they're hearing loud and clear the person presumably closest to you might be hoping to upgrade any day?? When some well-meaning, curious person asks you if you think you'll marry your co-habitant, they're really asking if the two of you will ever decide each other meets the standard. Are you ok with being viewed as sub-standard? And don't even start telling me that times have changed and it doesn't give that message anymore. Yes it does---$55 Billion dollars for the wedding industry, remember? People still see a life-long marriage as the end goal.

- Cohabitation increases the likelihood of divorce. Studies show the rate of divorce is 33 percent to 70 percent higher in couples who lived together before getting married. This might seem surprising; after all, isn't shacking up practice for marriage? Doesn't it "prove" if you can manage to live together you should be ready to marry? Well, no of course not, because a very poor foundation was laid. Two people who don't hold marriage in high regard, who don't respect the sacredness of sex and who've maintained for some time the other person isn't a "keeper"---gee what could go wrong with that? If a relationship is built with the belief the marriage license is meaningless, why does said license suddenly become meaningful ? The "house" was built on shifting sand. A house, like a lasting relationship, needs a firm foundation---concrete. There must be a concrete-solid respect for one another, self, and the institution of marriage for a marriage to work.

- Living together is not a commitment. It's not "a big step" and it's not a promise of a future. It's playing house, and it's silly. You can join the many voices that say it's an exclusive, lasting thing to celebrate and give a shower for (oh, pardon me while I vomit!), but it is a façade, nothing more. Jesus makes the distinction in his conversation with the woman at the well in John 4 when He lets her know He is aware she has had five husbands "and the one whom you now have is not your husband. " It must be important if He mentions it. Living together sans marriage is a selfish thing to do—"I want what I want but I don't want to actually commit, or work for something or honor something or someone." You shouldn't want anyone who would cohabitate. Further, you shouldn't want anyone who wants YOU if you are willing to cohabitate. Harsh. But true. You shouldn't want anyone with low standards of respect and value, nor should you want anyone who's willing to accept such low standards. That won't bring you the joy, security, comfort and happy companionship you're designed to have. Aim higher.

- The message cohabitation gives is not good for your future children, either. For example, if your teenage son knows that his mom and dad had such low standards of respect and honor for each other, is he really going to respect you as much as he would otherwise? Children see an example of how to treat their future mates by watching their parents interact. Be sure to give them the best example. Fathers, set the example that women are to be treated as precious beings. Mothers, make sure to model self-honor.
- For some unfathomable reason, my first husband told my children we lived together before we got married. We didn't, but they

believe him enough that I have lost credibility with them on the issue. Even though it's false information in this case, it's laid a poor example of the honor with which they should hold marriage and given them a faulty model. It'd be so much better for them to know that their parents had honored themselves, each other and the legal commitment. (It's just one of the reasons he's the ex. Sigh)

- Couples who marry as opposed to living together tend to be more educated and wealthier, and they build wealth more quickly. This is due to many factors, including the resistance of cohabiters to combine resources, for fear of a break-up. Another reason is couples who marry have learned the value of patience, hard work, stability and have the maturity to delay

> gratification and hold out for that which is meaningful. Don't be a bottom-dweller---be in the top tier! You can do it---get an education and a good career you can be proud of!

Okay latte drinkers, please come back now. We'll wait while you toss the napkin.

CHAPTER 23-- HAVE A RELATIONSHIP THAT'S FUN

There are so many important aspects to a healthy relationship—respect, integrity, shared goals and priorities, character, and on and on. It almost doesn't seem right to add "fun" as a requirement, right? But it it's not trivial at all. Fun is essential for our brains, our health, and our relational skills. Our brains are designed to release hormones when we are having fun that help us to learn, improve our energy, improve memory function, and all kinds of other scientific things beyond my ability to spell, much less explain. Suffice it to say we need the gift of fun in our lives and in our relationships.

The next big question then is what do you consider fun? In general, what types of activities do you enjoy or get excited about? What makes you laugh? When you're not working, taking care of the dogs and/or kids, and so forth, what do you find yourself doing? Are you usually active and high-energy in your pursuit of fun, or more likely to be doing a more stationary activity?

The obvious next question is how your concept of enjoyment and fun blends within your relationship? Not every joke will be hilarious to both people, and not every activity will be the best one ever for both people, but there should be a significant degree of similarity in how fun is defined and what's seen as enjoyable. If one person is an adrenaline junkie and the other likes to stay on the couch watching TV shows from the 70's, moving only to pet the cat or get a soda, that might not be a good blend. Finding mutual enjoyment, brain activity and growth will be a challenge. If on the other hand, both people are athletic and active, or both are 70's TV lovers, there will be a lot of fun happenin', lots of good memories made and lots of bonding.

Do you have a relationship where you agree on what an ideal vacation looks like? Do both of you like snowy mountains, or tropical islands, or short-term missions or......? Do you generally have the same sense of humor, and are entertained by similar movies or events? Of course not every activity one person loves will be even in the Top 10 of the other person's favorites, but there should be some mutual ground.

I didn't realize this importance when I married my current husband. I didn't notice that my husband's idea of perfect fun is so different from my own. I just assumed everyone loves the idea of vacationing around a body of water—the bigger the better—but I was quite wrong. He likes mountains, particularly snow-topped ones he can ski down, and is bored to tears on a beach. He can't do it. We can't share the relaxation of our toes in warm sand because he can't stand just sitting there. He can, however, sit in a car for literally 12-16 hours because he loves driving and seeing new sights from the highway. I cannot tell you how many thousands of hours I've spent in the passenger seat as we drive somewhere just for the purpose of driving. We don't actually do anything when we arrive. We usually spend whatever is left of the night in a hotel, then we pile back into the car the next morning. He is happy, refreshed, and recharged by this, while boredom tears have soaked my side of the car so much I feel like I have to pick my feet up off the floor or my socks will get ruined. I'm neither refreshed nor renewed when we get home. In fact I'm actually more exhausted and possibly resentful I can't get that weekend back. Our ideas of a pleasant evening are vastly different as well. Whereas I like spending the evening and weekend hours doing a productive project, doing something active, or learning something new, he is the reason I thought to mention "TV shows from the 70's" above. I'm thinking of entering a Perry Mason trivia contest. My preferences are not better than his, but they are quite different.

While this difference hasn't been a deal-breaker for us by any means, it's left gaps in our relationship. We don't often enjoy things together, and therefore don't bond over the happy memories we've made having fun together, since we generally don't. It's rather sad, and a big deficit I wish we considered before furthering our relationship so we could've formed a plan or agreed on a compromise.

Maybe the not-so-obvious next question is why fun is defined as it is, by both parties. Are there any red flags in this area? For instance, if one person loves to hunt because they enjoy the power they feel (not saying all hunters are power-crazed!) using a weapon and don't feel whole without one, or one person doesn't leave the couch because they're terrified of leaving the house, there are likely to be issues that need to be addressed. Less drastic, if one person is highly entertained by elaborate practical jokes but the other person sees these same jokes as mean efforts to harm or humiliate someone (which they are, by the way. Big red flag!), there may be reasons for a serious discussion.

Play Monopoly® together. Seriously. I suppose any board game would do, but I think Monopoly® is an excellent tool to gauge a person's aggressiveness, sense of fairness, level of competitiveness, rule adhesion or flexibility, money management skills and, even, maturity level.

It isn't possible for me to enjoy a game of Monopoly® unless every player has a color group, so I'll go to ridiculous lengths to make sure this aspect is covered and the playing field is level, at least in my mind. Once this is assured, I can quite happily demolish my opponents, but it is simply not fun for me unless everyone had an equal chance. This would probably be good information for a potential mate (when I was looking for one) or friend to have, as it speaks of my sense of fairness, willingness to help, possible co-dependency, et cetera. Playing with my daughter would tell her opponents she's far more interested in who's staying in the little hotels, or if the people who live in the house on Mediterranean Avenue are okay, rather than building a fortune or winning the game. Good to know: it speaks of her imagination, people skills, concerns, and possible lack of interest in amassing a fortune. She's a ton of fun and creativity, but she is probably not who an ambitious, wealth-oriented person wants on his team as a money-maker. Similarly, if said daughter was playing with an overly aggressive, ruthless, and selfish opponent, she may have reason to re-think the relationship or at least some facets of it; Is this guy a controlling, insensitive bully? There's much to be learned from a "fun" experience. Don't miss the lesson.

CHAPTER 24-- HAVE A RELATIONSHIP SURROUNDED BY HEALTHY, GOOD, SUPPORTIVE PEOPLE

You don't live in isolation. There are probably lots of people around you, like family, coworkers, friends, neighbors, fellow participants in your small group, other members of the clubs/organizations you belong to, etc. Since these surrounding people are a part of your life, they're a part of your significant other's life, and their surrounding people are part of yours. A huge factor in many marriages is the "surrounders." Hubby's mama can be a blessing or a nightmare, just like a father who spoils his daddy's-girl daughter can be a tough standard to contend with. Or that needy friend who calls at all hours could get in the way of privacy, rest and couple-time, or a friend can bring fun companionship and growth. It matters who's in your circle, and who's in the circle that will blend with yours if you share your life with someone.

The Book of Ruth provides a great example of an amazingly wonderful surrounder, Naomi. The book starts with the story of Naomi, a widow whose sons, tragically, also die and Naomi is left with only her daughters-in-law, Orpah and Ruth. (If I'm remembering right, I once heard Oprah Winfrey say her name was supposed to in fact be Orpah but due to a misspelling somewhere along the line, she is Oprah. Fun fact? Anyway....). We soon see the picture of Naomi's fabulous surrounder-ing. She released her daughters-in-law, whom she addresses as "daughters," from their obligation to make sure she gets safely to her people in Judah. She cared about their futures and wanted them to find husbands rather than travel with her to a land that isn't home to them. Orpah refused at first but then after another nudge did indeed go "back to her people and her gods" (v. 1:15), but Ruth refused to leave, in fact "clinging" to Naomi.

Imagine this. Naomi had cultivated a relationship with her sons' wives that compelled both women to commit to leave their homeland to make sure MIL was in good shape in her home. (Yes, Orpah bailed, but she did at least make the commitment!) I'm not sure of the laws or cultural traditions of the day, but I presume both Orpah and Ruth could've wiggled out of this journey, but they willingly went with her because of what Naomi had cultivated within their family. When I read The Book of Ruth, I imagine Naomi's family of six had Hallmark-commercial-like holidays and gatherings filled with genuine affection, respect, warmth, and everything that makes you want to buy a nice card. Nowhere in this story do we read about contention or discord. It appears that Ruth and Orpah had a "surrounder" they appreciated and adored, probably because she routinely put their interests ahead of her own and built them up long before her sons, their husbands, died. Awesome example!

Look carefully at the people on the fringes of your pre-marriage relationship and ask some important questions:

- Why are they there?
- What do they contribute to us?
- Should they be on the fringe of our relationship, or is it time for an adjustment?
- Do they contribute in a positive or negative way to the success and abundance of our relationship?

- Is a boundary needed? If so, which of us needs to set and communicate the boundary?
- Are these people likely to be like Naomi, building up loyalty and affection in the family?
- Are there secrets in the family? Why, and what are they?
- Is independence and autonomy encouraged and respected, or is there enmeshment somewhere?
- Are there chronic financial issues, with expected bailouts?

Who has your special person cultivated as part of her/his life? For that matter, who have you cultivated as a "surrounder?" We can't help what family we're born into, but as adults we absolutely can decide what family members to hold close and which ones to keep at arms' length—or even farther. Take a good look at the people you hang with on the weekends, who shows up on birthdays and whose name pops up on your phone screen. We all have "that" person we'd rather not have to deal with, but are they merely annoying or are they toxic? A relationship can survive a little toxicity, but too much and it's a goner.

I'm blessed with the best in-laws EVER. From Day One his family accepted me as their daughter and sister, allowing me to blend with their family as if I was born into it. There's never ever been a hint of toxicity, or resentment toward me, or side-taking against me. When I expressed gratitude and appreciation for this once to my mother-in-law, her shocked response was, "Well, what's not to like about you?" Oh, there's plenty, but she and her family choose to see me as her son does and therefore, they build up and encourage our relationship. In all honesty, I can't say for sure I would do what Ruth did and escort my MIL to her homeland because, well....it is Pittsburgh. But I greatly appreciate her positive contributions to the health of my marriage. Likewise, my friends-in-law (those friends of my husband who knew him before I came along) always include and encourage me because of their fondness for my husband, adding fun companionship and growth to our marriage. Without giving it conscious thought, these friends also contribute mightily to the health and stability of my marriage, which is exactly how it should be. I got lucky. I got great "surrounders."

My husband, on the other hand, got some questionable in-laws. Most of my huge family is very functional and congenial, many are Christians, and they adore him but there are some with questionable benefit to our relationship. We've had to make conscious—and usually fairly easy—decisions as to which family members to see a lot of, and which to keep at a healthy distance. There are 15 or so family members he will probably never meet! The godly, funny, kind ones are kept close while the occasional proud cheater and unrepentant addict are politely distanced. We just don't do much with the people we know we can't trust to surround us in a healthy, encouraging way. If history has shown a person to be a liar, a cheater or irresponsible, we've made that distinction and live accordingly as respectfully and politely as possible.

We're fortunate the people we've had to distance ourselves from were on the fringes anyway. What if there is a toxic person very close to your relationship? It's time to have some hard conversations and maybe make some tough choices regarding a boundary that's healthy and agreeable to both parties. This boundary might be that the person must call before coming over, or they don't get to take the kids every single weekend, or that, sadly, all contact is shut down until issues are dealt with and the person can be a safe contributor.

Another facet of the people surrounding you and your loved one is that, in the case of a –GULP—break-up, these are the people who'll have visitation or contact in some way with your children when you aren't present. This should be a very sobering thought. Hopefully this book, prayer, wise counsel, and good sense, prevents you from entering into a marriage that is not suitable, but things do happen, as the current divorce rate attests. Then what? Be sure to honestly consider the "surrounders" and decisions about their influence in your relationship and eventual family.

Listen to what your "surrounders" say. Do your friends think the two of you are a good match? You know your friends have formed an opinion. Ask them what it is and encourage them to be blunt and totally honest. What's the other person's family telling you about your mutual loved one?

Take a good, honest look at the people involved in your involvement. There really is NO fun in dysfunction, and it needs to be identified, called for what it is, and dealt with.

CHAPTER 25-- HAVE THE POTENTIAL FOR A COLSSIANS 3:18-19 RELATIONSHIP

As you know, Right Person/Right Relationship isn't geared toward those already married, thus the word "POTENTIAL" in this Chapter's title. Take a moment and carefully read the passage: "Wives, be subject to your husbands, as is fitting in the Lord. Husbands, love your wives and do not be embittered against them." (Updated New American Standard version). It basically is a two-verse, popping, concise how-to about building a good marital relationship. Although the verses are clearly meant for a husband/wife situation, I believe the verses hold wisdom that can stretch beyond these roles. I believe it's reasonable to glean the following:

- Women, understand and excel at your role.
- Men, be willing to be vulnerable. Do not enable bitterness to become your defense.

Simple, right? It actually should be, at first glance. Just 21 words, none over four syllables. THEN WHY IS IT SO HARD AND REQUIRES SO MANY BOOKS,

COUNSELORS AND TV SHOWS? If it's so simple, why can't we get it right?

Because we weren't made for this. Go back to Eve and Adam, the only known perfect relationship in human history. They were literally made for each other, perfectly fitted together with roles laid out: Adam was the leader and Eve was the helper. It was sort of a captain and first mate situation. Both roles are of utmost importance and are inter-dependent for the success of the voyage. It was a situation that produced only love and unity. But then all the bad things entered, and the ideal oneness was forever broken. So here we are... trying to make with our sinful selves what was made for sinless people. Kind of a square peg/round hole scenario. It just doesn't work and it can't be done. So, how do these two verses help?

First, let's get this out of the way---how many times have you heard this verse cited as "doormat" mentality-- that men are the big cheeses and are to dominate women who are commanded to put their heads down and do whatever the Cheese says to do? You've probably heard this multiple times as misquoted by nonbelievers and/or, God forbid, in a sermon. NOWHERE in this verse or in the entire Bible is this commanded by God, so please get that out of your head. Now.

Let's look, again, at Eve's creation. She was created as a suitable helper because Adam needed one. At that point in the story, we can assume equality, don't you think? At the time of Eve's creation God doesn't say "Okay guys, here's the deal—Adam, you da boss and Eve, you have nothing to say about anything he does." Quite the contrary. Eve's specific purpose was to a) Be a companion to Adam and b) Be a helper to Adam. I've never met, heard of, or read about a good helper that does nothing but follow orders, have you? To be a GOOD helper, one offers feedback and suggestions that are valuable, well-considered, and crucial to the progression of whatever project is being undertaken. Any good partnership is based on give-and-take, respect of opinions and movement toward a common goal. During the brief time the two of them had the perfect relationship, we can presume this worked well.

Then, the implosion. We can debate all day who started it, who did what first, etc., but the bottom line for our purposes comes in verse 16 of Genesis 3, where God decrees that part of the consequences of Eve's contribution to the implosion is that "(Your husband) will rule over you." Does this mean we're now in a Big Cheese/Doormat situation forevermore? I don't think so. God doesn't like oppression. I think it means the equality Adam and Eve have enjoyed is over. There now had to be a shift in the relationship, and someone had to assume the position of leader. This is bad for Adam as well. Now he is alone in his leadership and he doesn't know any better than Eve how to solve problems or do any other leader tasks. He sinned too, how's he supposed to lead this train?

I believe at this point Adam is under a load of responsibility which overwhelms him. He now must concentrate on his tasks, thereby he doesn't have the time and focus to live in the wonderful relationship with Eve and his Creator he had previously enjoyed. Thus, Eve is left desiring what she once had but now has lost. I believe the idea of God saying "You da boss, Adam" is a distortion of God saying "You guys blew the hierarchy I gave you. You decided to "be" Me and make your decision against what I told you, so now we have to re-arrange some things and have an authority structure. Adam, you get to be busy running some things. Eve, you'll be yearning for him because he won't be around as much and when he is around, he'll sometimes be stressed and cranky."

This leads us to the roles we've been left with now. Colossians 3:18 and 19 is full of rich, loving guidance about how to make the most of our roles now, and how to do them right. Understanding the verses, phrase by phrase and sometimes word by word, is key.

The first word in this passage is "wives." Obviously, a wife was first a woman, right? No one goes from infancy to full-grown wife without a lot of growth, so let's focus on that growth and what it ideally looks like. In our current culture, most women who become wives do so in adulthood; it's uncommon and illegal to have a child bride in the USA, thank God. It unfortunately happens in the world, but isn't the norm. I think we can assume the intended audience, the "wives" are of a reasonable level of maturity. The things of childhood such as brattiness, selfishness, and complete dependence have largely been put away. A woman becoming a "wife" can make a good choice of who to marry, ready to cooperate and assume her responsibilities. In other words, she's done the work in Part I and Part II of this book!

When joined to the next phrase of the passage, "be subject to your husbands," I believe there's an inference the wife in question has developed her own sense of individuality which now must be adapted to fit rightly with the husband. I'll now interrupt myself here for an important message:

*** Please note this is directed ONLY at "wives." Women are NOT directed to be in any way submissive to a man who isn't her husband! In no way, shape, or form I've ever found is there any Biblical direction that states women are inherently "less than" men and so should assume a lower standing. Sure, Old Testament culture was often demeaning to women, with men dominating them and minimizing their value, but this is not what God intended. We see His beautiful intention in the original equality between Adam and Eve when their relationship was still the ideal, perfect one. We also consistently see it in Jesus' dealings with women. The idea that men should and can dominate is man-made, often women-enabled, and purely human, not from God. If you're a woman who routinely bows to a man's assumed "superiority" you are out of line. Correct your thinking!

Okay, back to what I was saying before the interruption. A woman's individuality includes......well, anything she wants! It should include her appreciation and awareness of her talents, skills, preferences, and aptitudes. Her well-developed individuality includes her sense of humor, her communication style, her world view and opinions, and so forth.

So, presuming the "wife" is an adult woman with a well developed sense of herself, how does she become "subject" to her husband, and what does this have to do with our purposes in HAVING a right relationship? Huge question, way beyond my pay grade, but let's do the best we can.

First, what does it mean to be "subject?" I searched for quite a while to find a good definition and found some truly horrid ones which don't help our purposes, but I did land on one that I like—"To be under the wing of." Isn't that a wonderful picture of being subject to something? If I'm under the wing of someone, presumably I'm flying right along with them, heading in the same direction. I'm enjoying the same blue skies, but I'm protected from being the first to hit something head-on or some other bad occurrence. We can say we are "under the wing of our CEO" to which we are subject or "under the wing of our state laws" which we must follow. It isn't particularly objectionable to think of wives "under the wing of" their husband, if one chooses to have a husband, is it? It's a deliciously thrilling adventure for both the "wing-ee" and the "wing-er." One person is the lead flyer or pilot while the other one snugly is the co-pilot or companion. Both will arrive at the flown-to spot at the same time and in the same condition, and the journey was a peaceful one with roles comfortably assumed.

In a marriage, this being-under-the-wing thing is required, but what about in a friendship or close-but-not-married man/woman relationship? I believe the question, then, is one of ability and willingness to assume the under-wing position. Are you, female reading friend, willing to not always be the lead bird, directing the flight and responsible for the safety of all involved parties? This can be difficult, especially for so many of us who are independent, have lived our own lives and made our own decisions for decades. Soul-searching time—how good are you at calmly giving feedback with humility, then tucking under the wing of the lead bird (assuming he is flying in an ethical, safe manner of course. DO NOT 'fly' with an abusive, domineering, disrespectful bird. You're never called to do that!) and accepting leadership and protection instead of being the one in front with sword drawn?

Frankly, it never occurred to me until I spent a lot of time and money with marriage counselors during my first marriage that maybe I should've considered this under-wing thing more carefully. I was who I was—dominant, independent, overly self-assured in many ways. This didn't go so well in a bonded-forever (well that was the goal anyway. Ooops.) relationship with a human who maybe didn't want to constantly be bossed around. Who knew? On the other hand, this particular human didn't really want to take a strong leadership role, either. This means the two of us needed LOTS of work defining our roles prior to eating the wedding cake. If we'd done so, perhaps our children wouldn't have grown up with chaotic Christmas visitation times and tension during teacher/parent nights. If I had been wise enough to honestly look at the roles we both planned to assume, I would've understood the disaster into which I was heading, and adjusted accordingly. It's so very important to know your role, and whether you can—or even want to—adjust to it.

Second, why even discuss this in a book, when it isn't necessarily geared only toward marriage? Nice question, astute reading friend! It is important to consider WHAT and WHOM we're willing to subject ourselves to, before we find ourselves a subject! Everyone is subject to many things in life—bosses, teachers, banks, HOA's, traffic laws, Bible study leaders, coaches, and more. Some things aren't our direct, immediate choice. For instance, we're subject to our Federal, State and local laws unless and until we vote to change the law. Other things we can choose to subject ourselves to—or not. We have full control over what hobby groups we join, where we work, what we study and the ethics therein. We choose what groups of friends we have, and so on. It seems often we're subjects to something without even realizing it. Perhaps we don't want to be, or we're missing something we do want because we never took a moment to stop and think about it!

Take a moment to consider everything and everyone you are subject to, and ponder these things a bit. Do you want to be subject to the things you find yourself subject to? If not, can they be changed? For instance, if you're a US citizen you're subject to tax laws and there's probably not a lot you can easily do about that. But if you're an adult subject to your parents' house rules because you live in their home and want to make a change, you can! You most likely don't have to live under your parents' rules indefinitely, or your—gasp!—mother-in-law's rules forever. As an adult with awareness of who you are, you can decide to take whatever steps are necessary to allow yourself to not be subject to many things. Consider carefully whose wing it's appropriate for you to be under.

Women, we're almost done with your part of this passage, but not quite. The final phrase in verse 18 is “as is fitting to the Lord.” That means that God outranks the husband. A wife isn’t required to go along with any and all things her husband might want her to do. She must always follow God above all else. God designed marriage to “fit” a certain way, so He wants us to position ourselves accordingly. You follow Him first, therefore fitting yourself in the role. Again the question arises, “why are we discussing this in a book not necessarily geared toward marriage?” Because it’s vital to all women to know who they’re following.

Who, indeed, do you ultimately follow? We’ve seen all went well when humans followed God without veering from His path. There was perfection for them. We can no longer have perfection on Earth, but we do follow someone or something. Perhaps it’s our parents even though their time of control is long over, or it may be our own egos, the chase of physical beauty, or a desire for more money? These things--and all the other things on earth we might subject ourselves to—might have a place in our lives, but we need to determine who or what has the position of ultimate authority over what is 'fitting' for us. Make sure to fit in the spot the Creator made for you.

Once a woman has figured out what her role is in a marriage, how does she excel at it if she chooses to in fact be a "wife?" That, frankly, is the job of another book to explain. Remember, in Right Person/Right Relationship we're discussing how to best position yourself for a healthy and happy relationship. To that end, I hope this chapter has encouraged the female reader to ponder the role she's willing and able to take in a relationship. There may be adjustments to make, or things to accept and learn about how to excel in your important place as "First Mate."

Now, for the men's part of the Colossians passage, verse 19 of Chapter 3. Here we go, so hold on! Again, we're not talking about husbands in this chapter, but pre-husbands, if you will. We're considering the willingness and ability a man possesses, to be someone with whom a woman will HAVE a right relationship.

I was actually taken aback when I read this passage more closely a few weeks ago. I had always read the "love your wives" part, and it seems like an obvious command, but wait.... What is this "do not be embittered" thing?

Let's address the love issue first. Seems simple enough, right? But is it? Since men aren't generally strong when it comes to handling and expressing emotions—yes, I realize there are exceptions! I'm speaking generally and culturally here—it's not so easy for them. Though it may be difficult due to a man's wiring, he needs to be willing to be vulnerable, which is the base for a loving, intimate relationship. Terrifying, right?

Love cannot happen freely with a closed-off, overly-protected person.? That's surface, superficial affection at best. To be truly loving, there must be complete openness to letting another person into the secret areas of our hearts. Certainly not everyone should have this access; the guy you talk to in the break room at work sometimes on Fridays probably isn't the one to share your grief about your mom's passing when you were five years old. He's probably a fine guy but the basis for such sharing and openness probably doesn't exist in such brief encounters, so it's not an appropriate sharing. Openness and sharing are skills which must be learned and practiced to become wisely and thrillingly done. The key to my point is men, you must have a willingness to have the kind of vulnerability to share emotions honestly and appropriately, with enough self-assurance and maturity to know that

- You have chosen the receiver wisely and they can be trusted
- If this receiver turns out to not be true, you will survive.

While it'd be painful to be betrayed by someone you shared something deeply with, your heart needs to be able to say "Ouch, that hurt. I'll share again, but I've learned something about people from this experience." (Yes, hearts talk. Work with me here.) A betrayal does not and should not grant permission fora wounded man to seal off his heart.

Let's say that again---no hurt grants a man permission to seal off his heart, particularly if he wants to have strong, growing relationships. In the Colossians verse, men are directed to love, with no wiggle room. This directive doesn't say "sometimes" or "if they deserve it." Specifically men are instructed to love their wives, but since it's unreasonable to assume someone can be shut off completely and then magically open up to one person on their wedding day, we have to assume this is a process. Past hurts must be dealt with, and there may be walls of defense to break down.

Men, you must be willing to open your heart, lose the defensiveness, and be able to identify and appropriately express your emotions. I'm not talking about skipping through the house or office expressing every emotion you've experienced since you woke up on a rainy morning. I'm suggesting the only way to HAVE a strong, satisfying relationship is to get comfortable with your emotions, and be willing to appropriately extend them.

So, what does "love your wife" look like? Take that phrase word for word.

- "Love" means to put someone else's needs, feelings and well-being ahead of your own. This is and should be an area of life-long effort and growth.

- “Your” means the one you chose. The one you “bought” with time, energy, money, and emotions, just as she “bought” you. She belongs to no one else. She’s yours to cherish, protect, make laugh, build up, go on bike rides with, and anything that makes her know she’s loved by you.
- “Wife” is the ultimate unique human who is your suitable helper. She’s the one and only person on the planet who deeply supports you, thrills you with “that” look, knows your favorite foods and the ones you hate, learns to read your unspoken thoughts, depends on you, and trusts you. She is the only one who gets your attention, affection, and “that” look from you, and gets to rely on your protection, safety and provision. She’s the only

one to whom you give your body
and mind.

Almost overwhelming three little words from Colossians, yes? The adherence to those words, “Love your wife” is a life-long process. They require and deserve daily and unswerving commitment, or it isn’t love. Anything less than an unswerving commitment is a phase or a hobby. You’re gifted with the joy of having much more than that. You’re gifted with the responsibility of building love.

This brings us to the “bitterness” part. I mentioned I was surprised to see this word. Where did it come from? It seems out-of-the-blue in a sentence about loving your wife. It seems like a big jump from love to bitterness. Re-read the definition of “bitterness” in Chapter4. In case you didn’t, I’ll re-cap it for you. ”Bitterness” is defined as a lack of sweetness, and I believe it can lead to rage, resentment, depression, and a whole slew of other not-good things. No wonder we’re told not to have it and men specifically are told not to allow it in their closest relationship!

So just how did it get to be the sentence right after "love?" Probably because love, when betrayed and wounded, can produce massive pain which can result in a bitterness seed planted without your full knowledge or permission. A disappointment, betrayal, or harsh word can carry of the seed. A snide or thoughtless remark can threaten the core of our confidence, leading to a wall of bitterness to protect our heart from more threats. Sometimes as children our open little hearts are hit with venomous darts from parents, siblings, or others and we learn to build a wall of bitterness to protect us. We have to.

Did you know Isaiah 38:17 says "It was for my welfare that I had great bitterness"? I may be totally misunderstanding this verse, but I believe it may be saying that sometimes and in some circumstances it is beneficial to build walls up around our hearts, as long as we allow love to deliver us from the pit of bitter nothingness as the verse goes on to say. A child who grows up in an emotionally abusive situation, for instance, unfortunately must learn for emotional survival to let the barbs bounce off a wall. But eventually the child must grow beyond that bitter wall into an open-hearted softness which allows love to flow. I'm not suggesting that God wants us to build the bitterness, because bitterness is never a good thing, but I think He absolutely understands why we build the protection. I'm sure He hates the barbs that hurt us because it makes it harder for us to be who He created us to be, but He's not surprised by the bitterness left by those hurts.

So, manly reader friends, how are you doing with the preparation you must do to enjoy great relationships? Do you have walls of bitterness built up? Are they still strong and block off any possible threat to your very core? Well, it's time to tear those barriers down if you are want to have a loving relationship. This is probably terrifying, but true. The verse in Colossians is clear. You're to have no hurts, anger, resentments, or other blocks in your path to your wife and her path to you. This means the hard work of clearing that path must start long before you step into the role of husband.

Maybe you are thinking "I don't care what Colossians or anything else in the Bible says, I don't believe that stuff." Well, consider the wisdom of the verse. I can't imagine any sincere, connection-seeking man would disagree with the words, and think "Nah, it'll be a great thing to keep my defenses up with people, especially the one closest to me. That'll build the relationship I've always dreamed of! I'll feel so connected!" If you've been dreaming of a defensive, arms-length type of relationship, you really don't want a real one.

Technically, the verse says to not be embittered against your wife, but bitterness against anyone can quickly splash onto the closest person. Consider a scenario where your wife tells you to pick up your socks just like your mother did. Wifey is perfectly entitled to ask you to pick up after yourself, but if it reminds you of abuse from your mother because of socks, wifey is likely to get some misdirected bitterness splashed on her, isn't she? Not fair, and impossible to build a loving safe union with this bitterness.
Get rid of it.

Getting rid of all the bitterness and opening yourself to a close relationship may require a trained counselor to help you dig deep into the hurts that were the foundation for the seeds that built the wall.

I'm not going to lie,—sometimes this can feel like surgery without anesthesia. But if you genuinely want to be able to safely relate to someone heart to heart, ya gotta do it. Look around and find emotionally healthy, bitterness-free men. They exist, and they're happy. And their wives feel loved.

All righty, do you see what we've done in this chapter? We've examined the ideal of a close relationship, and discussed the importance of being personally prepared for your part of the ideal. This goes deep and could turn out to be a long process but it's hard to argue with its necessity. Any relationship with ill-defined roles and/or walls of bitterness will struggle. Mightily.

PART III-- CONCLUSION

This Part of the book is in some ways trickier and heavier than the others. Parts I and II deal mainly with who you are and what you want. Part III deals with the making and possible breaking of a relationship with another person. Adding another person is where things get exciting but complicated. What did you learn, ponder, or question? The next page is for any notes you might want to add, such as additional issues to discuss, questions to raise or re-planning ideas.

There's so much to consider when evaluating the rightness of a relationship because-- as I've said maybe a time or two-- no relationship can ever be perfectly right, so how can you tell if one is right enough? Especially given the thought that healthy humans grow, learn, develop, and change to some degree, how can you know you've found a connection worth keeping long-term? I'm going to take the wimpy and frustrating way through that question with a response of "you just know." Yes, that sounds flimsy and disappointing, but I believe in the vast majority of cases we have a deep sense of whether we're making a good decision about deepening a relationship with another person. We know it and feel it in our core. The trick is to learn to listen to yourself and your intuitions and trust them.

I've walked down the aisle twice and heard my intuitive heart loud and clear both times, and it was 100 percent accurate. The first time I knew as I walked toward the preacher it was a mistake. I had always known it deep down but never listened to my intuition or trusted it enough to make the tough decision to move on. Walking toward the preacher didn't seem like the appropriate time to backtrack because the mints and nuts were already paid for and it would be awkward to announce to the guests, but ohhhh how I wished for a decade and a half I'd adulted-up and valued myself enough to believe my intuition. The second time I walked down the aisle I knew it was a good move. I knew there would be issues to face and Lord A'Mighty, were there ever! But, after doing a lot of work I've shared with you, my intuition told me it was a solid connection and would take me and my daughters (the only good things to come out of Aisle

Walk #1!) to a good, exciting and worthwhile life. Again, intuition won out. We've had exactly that!

Learn to listen to yourself. Learn to hear what you perceive and register about the relationship, then be courageous enough to do what you're telling yourself to do, whether it's to deepen the relationship or let it go. You'll be so glad you listened to what your intuition says. There's no down side to doing so.

NOTES ON PART III

CONCLUSION

We did it! We finished our deep dive into the three components of a good, close relationship. We analyzed the strengths and weaknesses of the one perfect human relationship noted in history. We got terrifically honest and deep looking at ourselves, what we want and what we're willing to do to get it. I hope it's been an informative and worthwhile read for you, stimulating lots of thought and discussions. I also hope you worked hard making solid lists, and well thought out drawings to get you to your goal. If even one chapter or one sentence brought you closer to the relationship you were created to have, then it was worth your time and energy---and mine!

You worked hard and put in the effort required to complete Right Person/Right Relationship, You did, didn't you? If you didn't, GO BACK TO PAGE 1 and this time DO IT! Sheesh. You did it because you're ready to stop the frustrating, disappointing connections you've experienced in the past.

Does your completion of the book guarantee a perfect relationship? Sorry, no. Even the one that was perfect for a while couldn't maintain that level. We're each an example of imperfect humanity and when joining with other imperfect examples of humanity, we have no hope of the end result being ideal. But, if you intentionally and honestly look at these issues —and probably a few others we didn't touch in the book—you can greatly increase your chances of finding relationships that are enjoyable, safe, growing, and exciting. Wasn't that the reason why you picked up the book in the first place and carried it to the Cashier with equal amounts of hope and excitement and a "I hope no one sees me buying this. I can always say it's for my sister if anyone asks" trepidation? Everyone wants solid connections where we know we belong, and matter to another person. Hopefully now you're much better prepared and confident about finding and maintaining that type of connection!

Remember what you are worth, what others are worth, and go for the connection that appreciates, enhances, and protects that value!

Lift up your head and BE the most wondrous person you can be and go out there and FIND the person for the relationship you want to HAVE! You can do this!